Oxfordshire
MURDERS

NICOLA SLY

The History Press

First published 2010

The History Press Ltd
The Mill, Brimscombe Port
Stroud, Gloucestershire, GL5 2QG
www.thehistorypress.co.uk

British Library Cataloguing in Publication Data.
A catalogue record for this book is available from the British Library.

ISBN 978 0 7524 5359 0

Typesetting and origination by The History Press Ltd.
Printed and bound in Great Britain by
Marston Book Services Limited, Oxfordshire

CONTENTS

AUTHOR'S NOTE & ACKNOWLEDGEMENTS

The county of Oxfordshire is one of great contrasts. The bustling, cosmopolitan university city of Oxford, with its magnificent architecture, is renowned as one of the great seats of learning in the United Kingdom. Outside the city life is far more sedate, with much of the county comprising green spaces, small market towns and pretty villages.

In recent years, Oxfordshire has become almost synonymous with murder. Fortunately for the inhabitants of the county, these murders have been fictional ones, portrayed by actors in highly successful television crime dramas such as *Inspector Morse*, *Lewis* and *Midsomer Murders*. Yet, like any other county, as this collection of cases demonstrates, historically Oxfordshire has had its fair share of real life human tragedies, far removed from the world of entertainment, with lives lost needlessly through jealousy, greed, lust, hatred and madness.

Some of the cases recounted here were nationally reported, such as the 1931 murder of elderly widow Annie Kempson in Oxford. However, most were little known outside the county boundaries. These include the murders of three people and subsequent suicide of their killer in Shutford in 1935, the killing of 3-year-old George Hyde in Tetsworth in 1869, and the still unsolved murder of two little girls in Little Faringdon in 1893. Some of the perpetrators were undoubtedly insane at the time of their crimes, while others, such as the killer of 84-year-old Fanny Phillips at Woodcote in 1839, knew exactly what they were doing and had no regard for the inevitable consequences of their actions.

As usual, there are numerous people to be acknowledged and thanked for their assistance in compiling this book. Most of the material used was sourced from contemporary newspapers which, together with any books consulted, are listed in the bibliography at the end of the book. I must also thank the staff at the Oxfordshire Studies Centre in Westgate for their assistance in my research and the *Oxford Mail* for permission to use their photographs of victims Hilda Gibbs and Harold Matthews.

On a more personal level, I must also thank my husband, Richard, for his usual diligence in proofreading every chapter and for acting as chauffeur and occasional photographer on my research trip to the county.

Finally, my grateful thanks go to Matilda Richards, my editor at The History Press, for her continued help and encouragement.

Every effort has been made to clear copyright, however my apologies to anyone I may have inadvertently missed; I can assure you it was not deliberate but an oversight on my part.

Map of Oxfordshire.

1

'WHO WOULD GRUDGE TO SEND AN OLD FATHER TO HELL FOR £10,000?'

Henley-on-Thames, 1751

Mary Blandy was the only child of a lawyer, who also served as town clerk to his town of residence, Henley-on-Thames. Although Mary's mother had died, she lived comfortably with her prosperous father, Francis, in their home in Hart Street. However, by 1746, Mary had reached her late twenties without managing to attract a husband.

In an effort to redress this situation, Mary's doting father advertised a dowry of £10,000 for anyone who married his daughter. Not surprisingly, this attracted a large number of prospective suitors, all of whom were probably keener to lay their hands on the money than they were to lay their hands on Mary!

All but one of the men were considered and rejected, many of them refusing to consider marriage when Francis Blandy declined to advance them any money, saying instead that he would leave it to his daughter on his death. 'Such frequent Disappointments of Miss's Expectations, and natural Desires, undoubtedly raised her Resentment,' suggested the *London Evening Post*. (The fact was that although Blandy had advertised his wealth at £10,000, his actual worth was nearer to £3,000.) The only person who seemed a remotely suitable candidate was the Honourable Captain William Henry Cranstoun, the son of a Scottish nobleman, William 5th Lord of Cranstoun.

Hart Street, Henley-on-Thames, c. 1920. (Author's collection)

Captain William was more than twelve years older than Mary, a small man with a mean expression and a face permanently disfigured by smallpox scars. Nevertheless, his status made him a suitable prospect in the eyes of Francis Blandy and he obviously managed to charm Mary, since they began a courtship which was to last for more than five years. Only then was it discovered that Cranstoun was in fact already married and, not only that, but he also had a child.

Francis Blandy was most unhappy at this new turn of events and encouraged his daughter to turn her back on her intended husband. Yet Mary was by now deeply in love with William, who promised her that his first marriage was not legal, and she tried desperately to change her father's mind and make him see William as a suitable husband again.

William came up with a solution to their problems. He procured what he described as a 'love philtre' – powders which he gave to Mary to add to her father's food, to make the old man like him again. Unbeknown to Mary, the powders were in fact arsenic, a fact well-known to her lover who, it seems, would stop at nothing to get his hands on her fortune.

On the instructions of William, Mary added the powders to tea and oatmeal, which were then served to her father. Rather than having a change of heart about Cranstoun, Francis Blandy just became progressively more ill. The household servants also sickened, having eaten the remains of foodstuffs intended for their master. Fortunately they all recovered, but William's condition deteriorated until he was obviously near to death.

Hart Street and market place,
Henley-on-Thames, c. 1920.
(Author's collection)

Mary sent for his doctor, Anthony Addington, to attend him. Addington recognised that his patient had been poisoned and accused Mary of being responsible. At this, Mary panicked and threw Cranstoun's love letters onto the fire, along with the remaining powders. Servant Susannah Hall had the presence of mind to snatch some of the powder from the flames and it was sent to a chemist, who analysed it and found it to be arsenic.

Aware that he was dying, Francis summoned Mary to his bedside. Mary begged for his forgiveness, although she did not actually admit to poisoning him, only to administering 'love powders'. Francis Blandy willingly forgave her, urging her to say nothing to anyone on the matter for fear she might incriminate herself.

Even before her father's death on 14 August 1751, Mary was placed under virtual house arrest under the supervision of Edward Herne, the town's parish clerk. Confined to her bedroom, day and night, she craved her freedom and, on one occasion, when her bedroom door was inadvertently left open, she seized the opportunity to go for a walk.

However, once outside, she found herself mobbed by angry Henley residents, who eventually chased her over the Thames Bridge into Berkshire. Terrified by the hostile crowd, Mary was forced to take refuge with a friend, Mrs Davis, the landlady of the Little Angel Inn at Remenham.

An inquest was held into the death of Francis Blandy, at which the coroner's jury returned a verdict of wilful murder against Mary. She was arrested on 16 August and taken from the confines of her bedroom to the gaol at Oxford Castle to await her trial at the county assizes. Fears that she might try to escape led to her being forced to wear leg irons throughout her incarceration. Worse still, William Cranstoun completely deserted her and fled abroad, doubtless out of concern for the possible consequences of his own involvement in supplying the poison that had ultimately killed Francis Blandy. He is thought to have died in France in December 1752.

Mary's trial was held in the hall of the Divinity School at Oxford, since the normal location for the assizes, the Town Hall, was undergoing refurbishment at the time. The proceedings opened on 3 March 1752 before the Honourable Heneage Legge and Sir Sidney Stafford Smythe.

Oxford Castle, where Mary Blandy awaited trial. (Author's collection)

It was the first time that detailed medical evidence had ever featured in a trial for poisoning and, although Addington did not have the capability to analyse Francis Blandy's organs for the presence of arsenic, he was easily able to convince the jury that it had been arsenic that killed him.

Mary was defended by three counsels and also took the witness stand herself in her own defence. She claimed that she had believed that the powders she had given to her father were supposed to change his feelings against William Cranstoun and stated that she had not connected her father's illness with anything she might have administered in his food.

However, the Blandys' servants told a different story. They testified to having been ill after eating leftover food and to having seen Mary adding powder to her father's food and drink and later trying to burn the evidence. They also told the court of remarks she had allegedly made in their presence, calling her father 'a rogue, a villain, and a toothless old dog', and wishing him dead and 'in Hell'. She had even once asked, 'who would grudge to send an old father to Hell for £10,000?'

It took the jury less than five minutes to return a verdict of 'Guilty', after which she was sentenced to death and returned to Oxford Castle to await her execution. There, her warders were all very upset by her conviction – many local residents held the view that Mary was nothing more than a gullible dupe of Cranstoun, an innocent girl who would do anything for the man she truly loved. Mary was quick to dismiss the warders' concerns telling them, 'Don't mind it. What does it signify?' Professing herself to be hungry after her trial, she then tucked into a hearty meal of mutton chops and apple pie, her ordeal obviously having had no effect on her appetite.

In the six weeks between her trial and her execution, Mary spent her time in the condemned cell writing her own account of 'the affair' between herself and William Cranstoun. She also corresponded with a number of people, including a servant, Elizabeth Jeffries, who was herself waiting to be executed for her part in the murder of her master and his uncle.

The place of Mary's actual execution on 6 April 1752 is disputed, with some sources stating that she was executed in the grounds of Oxford Castle, others saying that a gallows was specially erected on Westgate. Regardless of the exact location, Mary faced her death with characteristic bravery, urging her executioners 'for the sake of decency, gentlemen, don't hang me high.'

The gallows took the form of a rope noose, which Mary had to climb a ladder to reach. With the rope around her neck, the hangman would turn the ladder, tipping Mary off and leaving her suspended by the neck until dead. Still protesting her innocence, Mary clutched a prayer book in her hands. It was agreed that she would drop the prayer book as a signal that she was ready to die and, when she had finished her prayer, the book was dropped and Mary died instantly.

Her body was carried back to the castle by six men and she was later buried at Henley parish church, between the graves of her mother and father. Her ghost is said to haunt both Westgate and the Little Angel Inn.

2

'SOMEBODY CRIES MURDER!'

Forest of Wychwood, 1824

Brothers Joseph and James Millin were both in service as gamekeepers to Lord Churchill, on his Blenheim estate in West Oxfordshire. On the evening of Tuesday, 15 June 1824, the two men were out patrolling an area called Hensgrove Copse, within the Forest of Wychwood. The brothers had separated and, at about half past eight, Joseph took a single shot at a rabbit. Roughly fifteen minutes later he heard a shot from another part of the forest, accompanied by a shout of 'Halloa!'

Joseph went to investigate and, within minutes, came across two men, William James and Henry Pittaway, who had also heard the shot and were hurrying in the direction of the sound.

'Have you shot?' William James asked Joseph, who replied that he had.

'We heard someone shout "Halloa",' William continued.

'I thought the cry was murder,' added Pittaway.

William James seemed to know where the shot had originated from and said that he believed the voice he had heard shouting was that of Joseph's brother, James. Soon, the three men came upon James Millin, lying on the forest floor, badly wounded.

'My thigh is broken. I am shot,' James told his brother, adding that it had been poachers who had shot him.

Unbeknown to his brother, James Millin had already been found by a local farmer, Mr Thomas Young, who had immediately rushed off to get help. When Young returned with several other people, he found Joseph Millin, William James and Henry Pittaway trying to stem the flow of blood from the shot man's left thigh.

Blenheim Palace, where Joseph and James Millin were gamekeepers to Lord Churchill. (Author's collection)

The wounded gamekeeper was carried to Joseph's home, South Lawn Lodge, on the estate, where in spite of the attentions of a doctor, he died at eleven o'clock that night. A later post-mortem examination, carried out by surgeon Mr Augustus Batt of Witney, showed that the femoral artery in his thigh had been perforated and, as a result, he had bled to death.

At daybreak the next morning, Joseph Millin went to the spot where his brother had been shot and searched the area carefully. Roughly 10 yards from where James had fallen, Joseph found two sets of footprints, along with some burning to the leaves of surrounding bushes, which he believed was caused by the gunpowder from a shotgun. On one bush, there were small pieces of wadding from a shotgun cartridge. Joseph traced the trajectory of the shot from the bushes and found two leaden balls.

Having been in the area at the time of the shooting, William James and Henry Pittaway were naturally prime suspects in the murder of James Millin and were questioned at great length by the police. However, no evidence could be found to link them with the murder and they were eventually discharged, leaving an inquest held by coroner Mr W. Macey to record a verdict of 'wilful murder against some person or persons unknown'. James Millin, who left a wife and child, had only been employed as a keeper for a short time and it was theorised that he might have been mistaken for his brother, Joseph, who had previously been very active in the detection and prosecution of any poachers found on the estate.

Whichever of the brothers the shot had been intended for, Lord Churchill wasn't about to let the matter rest. He contacted Sir Richard Birnie, the Chief Magistrate at Bow Street, and requested the services of a Bow Street Runner and William Salmon was sent to Oxfordshire to assist in the search for the gamekeeper's killer.

Salmon's first action was to carry out another search of the area where James Millin had been shot and a third ball was found, which was thought to be the very one that had passed through the victim's thigh. The Bow Street Runner then began a careful and thorough investigation of the events of the night of 15 June, starting with the two previously discharged suspects, Henry Pittaway and William James.

Both Pittaway, who was twenty-five years old and James, who was forty-eight, had previous convictions for poaching. Not surprisingly, several people had seen them in Wychwood Forest around the time of the shooting, although nobody had seen either man carrying a gun. Pittaway's house had already been searched after the murder and his gun examined in comparison with one of the lead balls found by Joseph Millin. Although various poaching tools were found, including hare nets, deer slips, a powder horn, a bullet mould and a gun, the ball had been so deformed by striking the ground that it would not fit either Pittaway's gun or the bullet mould.

Several people stated that William James had often threatened violence towards the Millins, on account of a previous summons that he had received for poaching. William was given a sheep by a local farmer, which he jointed and hung on the beams of his cottage. Joseph Millin and his then assistant, John Bayliss, saw the meat and, believing it to be venison, took a summons out on William James who was forced to appear before the local magistrates. However, before his case came up, Bayliss left his job and consequently nobody appeared at court to give evidence for the prosecution and William James was discharged. After the inquest had closed, one witness allegedly heard William James say, 'Revenge is sweet and let the Lord repay it.'

At around midnight on the night of the murder, James and Pittaway had gone to the Hit and Miss public house, where they had related the story of James Millin's 'accident' to a fascinated audience of drinkers. William James had mentioned that they had seen a man in a light coloured coat or smock running from the scene of the shooting but had not caught up with him. Mr Sims, one of the drinkers at the pub that night, visited William James at home on the following day. William's wife told him that she expected their house to be searched in connection with the murder and asked Sims to take a gun and hide it. He had placed it in his barn but, a few days later, he became nervous and asked Mrs James to take the gun back, which she refused to do. Sims then hid the gun under some straw in a barn belonging to somebody else and, when it was eventually retrieved, it was found to be loaded with three balls. Pittaway's gun was dismantled after the murder and he too took his weapon to a friend's house for safe keeping, retrieving it only after he had initially been apprehended and discharged.

Now, Salmon compared the new ball found in the forest with the bullet mould found at Pittaway's house and was positive that the two matched. As a consequence, William James and Henry Pittaway were arrested again and formally charged with the wilful murder of James Millin. Protesting their innocence, they were brought before magistrates, where they were committed for trial at the next Oxford Assizes.

The trial was conducted by Mr Justice Park, with Mr Taunton prosecuting and Mr Curwood defending. As the jury was being sworn in, the defence objected to three members, who were promptly replaced.

The evidence against the two defendants seemed sparse and the essence of the case boiled down to three main factors – their presence in the locality on the night in question, the bullet mould found at Pittaway's house and various comments they had both made before witnesses about the murder.

That the two men had previous convictions for poaching and had been in the forest on the night of the murder was not in dispute, since they met Joseph Millin and helped to carry the victim back to Millin's house. The fact that none of the witnesses had seen either man carrying a gun that night was largely ignored. William James and Henry Pittaway stated that, on the evening of the murder, they had been inspecting Pittaway's potato field when they had heard shooting and a cry for help. 'Somebody cries murder!' remarked Pittaway and the two men had run towards the sound of the shot, meeting Joseph Millin on their way.

Much weight was placed on remarks that William James and Henry Pittaway had made both before and after the murder. Many of these comments seem to have been heard by members of the Pratley family and James, George, Job and Philip Pratley all testified in court, mostly about what had allegedly been said by the defendants.

Job Pratley had heard William James say, 'If one man could have an opportunity, Millin would not be keeper much longer.' William had later remarked to Philip that he would '... no more mind shooting Millin than nothing, if he could get the chance, and was sure no one was with him,' and that he was '... sure murder would be done this summer.' James Pratley had overheard a conversation between his brother, George, and William James on the day after the murder when William had been taken into custody for the first time. 'My neck is but short now. Perhaps it may be longer at Midsummer,' said William.

The Pratley family were not the only people who had heard the defendants talking about the murder. John Hodgkins heard the two men discussing the case during the inquest and told the court that they were under the impression that, if only one man had actually pulled the trigger it would be impossible for two men to be hanged. Then there was also the 'Revenge is sweet' comment made by William James after the inquest.

The third factor in the case against James and Pittaway was the fact that the lead balls found in the area, including the one that had apparently killed James Millin, appeared to have been fashioned in Pittaway's own bullet mould.

Once the prosecution had rested, Mr Curwood, the counsel for the defence, stated that he had no witnesses to call and, as the two accused men declined to speak in their own defence, it only remained for Mr Justice Park to summarise the evidence for the jury. Much of this summary focused on the fact that two men were charged with the murder when only one man had actually pulled the trigger and fired the fatal shot. Park informed the jury that all who were present at the time were, both legally and morally, equally responsible for the murder.

The jury took only fifteen minutes to return a verdict of 'guilty' against both defendants and Mr Justice Park donned the black cap preparatory to imparting sentence of death upon them. However, neither defendant took the sentence lightly and every time the judge opened his mouth, William James shouted over him.

'Prisoners at the bar, you have been found guilty...' began the judge.

'I am not guilty, so help me God,' interjected William James.

'...and after a full, fair and impartial trial...'

'It was not impartial.'

'...by a jury...'

'A pretty jury indeed.'

'...you have been found guilty...'

'We are both innocent. We had no gun and I had no gun that day.'

'...of a most horrid murder...'

'Murder! We did not do the murder, my Lord. I declare again, we did not.'

Eventually, the judge managed to complete his pronunciation of the death sentence, ordering that both men should be executed, following which their bodies should be anatomised by surgeons. William James continued to argue his every word and Henry Pittaway eventually added his own voice, first urging his co-defendant to say no more, then reiterating his own innocence. Urged to repent by the judge, James shouted, 'I cannot repent of what I am not guilty.'

The two men had just a few days to languish in Oxford Castle awaiting their execution, during which time both continued to assert their innocence of the crime. Given that both now faced certain death, it is interesting to note that at no time did one of the men try to save his own neck by implicating the other, especially as only one of them could have fired the fatal shot.

They maintained their innocence until the very last, even in the face of exhortations from the prison chaplain to repent and seek mercy '... at the throne of grace'. As they stepped calmly onto the scaffold on 2 August 1824, William James even joked as the noose was placed around his neck, saying, 'The rope is tight enough for me already but I suppose it will soon be tighter.'

Although both men insisted that they had not committed the murder, after their execution the contemporary newspapers mysteriously reported, 'We are informed from those who had much conversation with them since their condemnation that there is no doubt but they were the persons who committed the murder and that their sentence was a very just one.' Since the newspapers do not elaborate further, it is not possible to make a totally informed decision about the guilt or innocence of either Henry Pittaway or William James.

Unfortunately, one fact about the murder and subsequent executions that is not in dispute is that three wives were left widows and a total of nine children were left fatherless.

3

'I'LL SEE HER DAMNED FIRST'

Oxford, 1827

In recent years, Brasenose College in Oxford has become closely associated with murder, being the fictitious 'Lonsdale College' of the long-running television police drama *Inspector Morse*. However, back in 1827, the college was central to a real-life murder mystery of its own, one that has remained unsolved to this day.

Ann Crotchley (also known as Ann Crutchley, Priest, Price or Preece) was a young, unmarried woman described in the newspapers of the day as being 'of great personal beauty'. The twenty-four-year-old woman came from a respectable Herefordshire family but was brought to Oxford by a lover who, having first seduced her and ruined her reputation, abandoned her in the city with no friends or means of supporting herself. Too ashamed to return home, Ann resorted to prostitution, although she was said to be '...far beyond the class of such unfortunate outcasts'.

At the beginning of December 1827, Ann met a fellow prostitute, Harriet Mitchell, and the two young women quickly became firm friends. Walking the streets of Oxford together on 6 December, Ann and Harriet came across a riotous drinking party being held in the ground floor room of a student of Brasenose College. As the two girls passed, they were called to the window by the students and asked if they would like a drink. Both Ann and Harriet asked for wine but were told that there was none. However, one third-year student, Houstonne John Radcliffe, told the girls that he would give them some brandy if they would drink it. Ann and Harriet agreed that they would. The window was barred, hence it was not possible to pass either a glass or a bottle from inside the room to the street outside. Thus Radcliffe filled a large teapot with brandy and both girls drank from the spout, with Ann consuming an estimated pint of spirits.

Brasenose College, Oxford. (Author's Collection)

Not surprisingly, she soon became extremely intoxicated. The women parted company and Ann was later found collapsed in the street, on a doorstep in Blue Boar Street. At fifteen minutes past midnight on 7 December, John Hedges, a porter from All Saints' College, arrived home to find her slumped unconscious in the doorway of his house, her head on the doorstep and her feet in the gutter. Hedges knocked on his door, and, when his servant James Champ responded, the two men carried Ann to a passage at the side of the house and propped her against a wall in a seated position. At the time, neither Hedges nor Champ saw any sign of an injury to the inebriated woman and, leaving Champ to watch over her, Hedges went off in search of a watchman – a forerunner of the modern police constable.

He first found Harriet Mitchell engaged in conversation with a young apprentice tailor named Richard Llewellyn who, having heard her squealing and laughing in Oxford High Street, had gone to see if she was all right. Hedges approached Harriet and her companion to ask if they had seen a watchman and Harriet, recognising her friend Ann from Hedges's description of the drunken woman, offered to see her home safely. Ann had lodged with watchman James Cox and his wife Mary Ann in the St Thomas's area of Oxford for almost four months.

By the time Hedges got back to his home, he was accompanied not only by Harriet and Llewellyn but also by a watchman named Richard Field and another passer-by, painter John Williams. Field seemed quite disinterested in the plight of the unfortunate young woman. Asked to take Ann into his watchman's box – the small building that provided shelter for the town's watchmen – he immediately refused, saying, 'No. I'll see her damned first,' and walked away. He was later to mention Ann's predicament to almost everyone he met on his rounds of the town that night.

With Field prepared to offer no practical assistance, Harriet and Richard Llewellyn took it upon themselves to get Ann back to her lodgings. With the assistance of John Williams, they hauled Ann to her feet but found her completely incapable of standing

Blue Boar Street, where Ann Crotchley was discovered in a doorway. (© N. Sly)

upright. Harriet asked Williams to stay with Ann while she and Llewellyn found a barrow in which to wheel her home and Williams agreed although, doubtless wary of being abandoned in charge of a drunken woman, he told them that he would only wait for an hour.

Meanwhile, Field mentioned to Esther Stimpson and Maria Burley that there was a woman who was 'very tipsy' lying in Blue Boar Street. Esther and Maria went for a look at the spectacle and found Ann lying senseless on the ground, her petticoats up to her knees and her cap missing. Williams was standing close to her and told the ladies that he was waiting for Ann's friends to transport her home.

Field also mentioned Ann's situation to another watchman, Anthony Cromwell. Cromwell went to see Ann at just after one o'clock in the morning, finding her lying apparently asleep in the alley, with John Williams still standing guard over her. Fifteen to thirty minutes later, he met Williams about 150 yards from where he had last seen him with Ann. Williams had obviously tired of waiting and was now walking away. When Cromwell asked him how Ann was, Williams replied that she was 'just the same as when you left her' and continued on his way. Cromwell went back to check on Ann and found that this was indeed the case.

Richard Field and Cromwell met up again at about two o'clock in the morning, and checked Ann together, at which time she was still alone, sitting propped up against the wall in the passageway, either deeply asleep or unconscious. Field subsequently told watchman John Cox about Ann and, when Cox went to check, he found a very different scenario. Ann was lying in the passage, a large pool of blood glistening around her in the moonlight. The clothes on the lower half of her body seemed to be drenched in blood and Cox believed that she was dying.

Only now were the watchmen galvanised into some sort of action. When Cox reported his findings to Field, the two men procured a wheelbarrow and, with the assistance of Anthony Cromwell, they wheeled Ann to the home of apothecary Mr Simmonds, who advised them to take the young woman straight to the hospital.

Oxford High Street, 1920s. (Author's collection)

For reasons known only to themselves, the three watchmen ignored his advice, instead taking Ann to her lodgings and leaving her in the care of her landlady, Mary Ann Cox. Field then went back to see Mr Simmonds and asked him to call round and examine Ann but Simmonds refused, telling Field to consult Mr Dickerson, the parish doctor. Dickerson agreed to attend and went to visit Ann at her lodgings at about five o'clock on the morning of 7 December. Landlady Mary Ann Cox was used to her lodger coming home 'tipsy' and had simply laid her on some blankets in front of the fire to sober up, before going upstairs to her bed.

When Dickerson knocked on the door of the house next door by mistake, Mary Ann dismissed him from her bedroom window, telling him that Ann was merely drunk and did not need the services of a doctor.

Shortly afterwards, Mrs Cox became aware of Ann groaning piteously downstairs, at which she got a lantern and examined the girl more closely. She found that Ann was bleeding heavily from her 'women's parts' and that she appeared to have lost a great deal of blood. In response to Mrs Cox's questioning, Ann was only able to say that she had been 'ill-used' by a man, but that she did not know who he was.

Mr Dickerson was quickly summoned back to the house, arriving at about eight o'clock to find Ann bleeding heavily from her womb and almost insensible from loss of blood. Dickerson could find no external injuries to account for the bleeding and was able to do little for his patient. When he returned to the house on the evening of 7 December, it was to find that her condition had worsened considerably and, at about two o'clock in the morning of 8 December 1827, Ann Crotchley died.

As there were no signs of any external injury to the young woman, Mr Dickerson was concerned that she might have been poisoned and decided that it was necessary to perform a post-mortem to determine the true cause of her death. Later that day, Mr James Paxton, an Oxford apothecary and surgeon, assisted Dickerson in carrying out an examination on the dead woman. They found her body to be covered in recent bruises, the blackened marks on her left arm, breast, legs and thighs standing out in sharp contrast to a body made pale through loss of blood. The cause of her death was determined to be haemorrhage from two deep cuts and the surgeons surmised that a knife or other sharp instrument had been violently thrust into her vagina, causing the lacerations. One of the cuts was between 3 and 4in long, a ragged, gaping wound, which was deep enough to accommodate the entire length of one of surgeon James Paxton's fingers. The other wound was only slightly smaller and less penetrating.

An inquest was convened at the Three Crowns Tavern, St Thomas's, before city coroner George Cecil. The jury was taken to see the body of Ann Crotchley and remarked that the woman was 'the most handsome they had ever seen', having the '...most perfect symmetry and delicacy of limbs'. The jury saw the bruise marks on Ann's left breast, which were believed to have been caused by pressure from the four fingers and thumb of a man's hand. There were similar marks around Ann's ankles and it was thought that two 'monsters' had cruelly held the girl down, while a third inflicted the fatal injuries on her body.

Having heard from everyone who was known to have encountered Ann Crotchley in Blue Boar Street in the early hours of the morning of 7 December, the coroner called John Williams to give evidence. Mr Cecil made it quite clear to Williams that he was under suspicion of murdering Ann and that he was not therefore obliged to answer any questions put to him by the jury, particularly any that might incriminate him in the young woman's death. So cautioned, Williams was asked to give his account of the events of 7 December.

Williams's statement matched those of all the other witnesses who had already testified. He had been a mere passer-by and had been motivated by humanity to help Ann. Williams said that he had offered the watchman a shilling to carry her home but the watchman had refused. In the face of such blatant indifference from a person in authority, Williams had felt that he had no option other than to help Ann himself. He had agreed to take care of her while her friends had been searching for a means of transporting her home and had only left her when he believed that they had abandoned her, at which point he had felt it necessary to seek further assistance. (The coroner did not pick up on the fact that Williams had encountered watchman Anthony Cromwell shortly after leaving Ann and made no request for his help.) Williams assured the coroner's court that he knew nothing at all about how Ann had been injured and that he was completely innocent of having done anything that might have harmed her in any way.

Having given his evidence, Williams was dismissed while the coroner summed up the case for his jury. Cecil said that it was beyond any reasonable doubt that Ann

Crotchley had come by her death as a result of the injuries documented by the doctors and, as it was impossible for her to have inflicted those injuries herself, it was also beyond all doubt that she had been brutally murdered. Cecil told the jury that it was therefore their job to determine whether or not they could safely say by whom the murder had been committed.

Although John Williams was under suspicion simply because he was the person who had had the most opportunity to commit the atrocities against the victim, the evidence against him was so scant that no jury in the world would ever convict him of the crime based on that evidence.

The jury retired for several hours, returning to tell the coroner that they were unable to agree on their verdict. While they all agreed on 'wilful murder', they were almost equally divided between verdicts of 'wilful murder by John Williams' and 'wilful murder by some person or persons unknown'. Since there was a small majority in favour of the latter verdict, it was this that was eventually recorded by the coroner. With the prime suspect now seemingly exonerated by the coroner's court, the city of Oxford and the university each offered a reward of 100 guineas for the apprehension of the murderer or murderers.

Ann Crotchley was buried in the cemetery at St Thomas's before a large crowd of mourners, most of whom had not known her in life but had been drawn by morbid curiosity to witness her funeral. Her grieving mother travelled from Hereford to Oxford to escort her daughter's coffin. However, Ann was not to rest undisturbed in her grave for long.

Just twelve days after her death, Ann's body was exhumed so that a second post-mortem examination could be carried out. The authorities had received an unprecedented number of letters expressing outrage at the barbarity of her murder, the majority of which were anonymous. Such was the public outcry at the case that it was felt that there was no alternative other than to re-examine the body of the unfortunate victim in an effort to gain some further insight into who might possibly have killed her in so ghastly a manner. It was also rumoured that the exhumation was ordered as a result of pressure from Brasenose College who, having made their own investigations into the murder of Ann Crotchley, wanted to ensure that her death had not resulted from the excessive amount of brandy given to her by student H.J. Radcliffe. Radcliffe, who had already admitted giving Ann intoxicating liquor, hurriedly left Brasenose when Ann's death was first publicised.

At a disciplinary hearing against him, held in his absence by the college on 31 January 1828, he was formally excluded from the college until 'after the long vacation'. However, he was never to return to his studies and, less than two years after Ann's death, the college were notified that he had died.

The second post-mortem examination on Ann's body, carried out by Professor J. Kidd, the professor of anatomy at Oxford University, along with surgeons James Paxton, C. Wingfield and W. Tuckwell, confirmed the results of the first. Aside from her terrible internal injuries, Ann had been a perfectly healthy young woman, with no signs of any natural disease. Her death had resulted from blood loss following the insertion of either a sharp instrument or a blunt and powerful instrument into her vagina, the instrument then having been violently jiggled in different directions, causing deep cuts.

It was unthinkable that the perpetrator of so gruesome and violent a murder should go unpunished and, as John Williams was so far the only possible suspect, he had been detained in the Bridewell gaol pending the results of further enquiries. Once the results of the second post-mortem were known, the town magistrates – John Hickman (the then mayor of Oxford), Sir Joseph Locke, Alderman Parsons and Messrs Wootten, Robinson, Slater and Ensworth – assembled in the town clerk's office at the Town Hall to discuss their next actions.

Until then, much of the investigation into the murder had been conducted privately. However, John Williams was understandably keen for the investigation to be made *coram populo* – in the public eye, rather than behind closed doors. At their meeting, the magistrates resolved that this should be done and, as a consequence, Williams was brought before them to publicly give his own account of the last hours of Ann Crotchley's pitifully shortened life.

Williams was a native of Oxford, about thirty years old and described as 'of genteel appearance'. He worked as a picture framer and, apart from the normal behavioural misdemeanours associated with men of his age – presumably amounting to little more than occasionally drinking to excess and perhaps some fighting – was of previous good character. During his appearance before the magistrates, he possessed all the confidence of innocence and it was difficult to view him as a serious suspect for the murder. Indeed, the entire hearing eventually degenerated into something of a theatre, with the authorities struggling to keep control of the hordes of spectators who had assembled for the show. It was only the committal of one of their number to prison for contempt of court that brought about the realisation to the crowd of the seriousness of the proceedings.

The only real evidence implicating John Williams in the murder of Ann Crotchley was the time he had spent alone with her in the street and some faint red stains on his coat sleeve, which might or might not have been blood. Williams offered two possible explanations for the stains. Shortly before the murder, an unknown assailant attacked him in the street. The two men had fought and, according to Williams, he had 'drawn claret' from his attacker, who had then fled. Additionally, Williams suffered from a weakness of one wrist following a bad sprain and occasionally bound it up using a length of wide, red ribbon, the colour of which frequently transferred to his clothes when the dye ran in wet weather. Williams was able to provide witnesses, both to the fight and to the fact that he sometimes supported his wrist with a red watch ribbon.

At the conclusion of the hearing, the magistrates were left in an impossible situation. There was insufficient evidence against Williams to commit him for trial at the next assizes but, apart from Williams, there was no viable suspect for the horrific and very public crime that had been almost the sole topic of conversation in Oxford since it had first been committed. Thus a decision was made to authorise Williams's release on bail, although, deliberately or not, the bail was set at £500, a figure too high to be within the means of the prisoner, who was returned to jail pending either receipt of bail or the commencement of the next Quarter Sessions of the assizes in Oxford.

The Quarter Sessions opened on 14 January 1828 and the case of John Williams was placed before the Grand Jury, whose task it was to consider the indictment against the defendant, hear the statements of key witnesses and determine whether or not Williams should stand trial.

The written indictment stated that John Williams, described as a carver and gilder, '... not having the fear of God before his eyes but being moved and seduced by the instigation of the devil, on the 6th day of December in the year of our Lord 1827 did, in and upon one Anne Crotchley ... feloniously, wilfully and with malice aforethought make an assault ...'.

Since this assault had resulted in mortal wounding, it was further indicted that '...the said John Williams did feloniously, wilfully and of his malice aforethought kill and murder the said Anne Crotchley against the peace of our said Lord, the King, his crown and his dignity.' The indictments were repeated word for word using the victim's alternative names of Ann Preece and Ann Priest.

The Grand Jury heard from all the witnesses involved, with the exception of Williams himself, this being a hearing to determine whether or not he should be tried for his supposed part in the death of Ann Crotchley. Since a defendant in England is always presumed innocent, the Grand Jury heard only testimony from what would be witnesses for the prosecution, as it would be the job of the prosecution to prove Williams guilty, rather than that of the defence to prove him innocent. Also taken into consideration by the Grand Jury was the fact that, if Williams were tried and acquitted due to lack of evidence, there was no possibility that he could be tried again for the same offence, even if more concrete evidence against him emerged in the future.

Having heard the paucity of evidence against John Williams, the Grand Jury determined after several hours of private deliberation that there was no true bill against him. Williams was not tried for the murder of Ann Crotchley, either then or at any time in the future, and neither was any other person. The large rewards offered for the capture of the murderer or murderers went unclaimed and the murder remains unsolved to this day.

Note: In various contemporary accounts of the murder, the name of the mayor of Oxford, who headed the magistrates' enquiry into the murder, is given as both Mr Hickman and Mr Hickson. There is also some confusion about the names of the watchmen involved in the case. It is not absolutely clear whether there are two different watchmen, John Cox and James Cox, or if James Cox, who was both a watchman and landlord to the victim, has been mistakenly named John in some newspaper accounts. It seems more probable that there were two watchmen both named Cox.

4

'HE MUST HAVE POSSESSED ALMOST HERCULEAN POWER'

Wantage, 1833

At about six o'clock on the morning of 31 August 1833, the twelve-year-old stepson of the landlady of the White Hart Inn, in Newbury Street, Wantage, woke up and went downstairs. Unusually, the pub was still in darkness and the child's first thought was to open the window shutters to let in some daylight. As he crossed the kitchen, he stumbled over an object on the floor and, only when the shutters were opened, did he realise that the object he had tripped on was the severed head of his forty-year-old stepmother.

Anne Pullen was a widow with two children, a boy and a girl, who also had custody of her late husband Richard's child with his former wife. Since her husband's death, Anne had kept the pub on her own, without assistance from any servants. On 30 August, the three children had gone to bed at about nine o'clock, leaving their mother alone to deal with her customers. Now she lay dead by the fireplace, her head adjacent to her feet, seemingly swept from her body by a single stroke of a sharp instrument. A pocket containing her purse and some coins had been torn from her dress.

The neighbours were alerted by the boy's bloodcurdling screams and one, Mr Poskin, rushed to see if he could help. One look at the blood-drenched room and the condition of the body of his neighbour convinced him that he could do nothing apart from removing the surviving children from the premises and summoning the police.

*Market place,
Wantage, 1950s.
(Author's collection)*

*Newbury Street,
location of the White
Hart Inn where
Anne Pullen was
murdered.
(© N. Sly)*

Almost immediately, the police were told about the strange behaviour of a man in another of the town's public houses on the night of the murder. He was George King, a labourer from Cunmor, near Oxford, who worked in the bean fields at nearby Letcombe.

The previous night had been very rainy and windy and yet, at ten o'clock, King had strolled into the Blue Boar carrying a 'bean hook', with his coat over his arm '...as though it had been in the meridian of the hottest day in summer.' King had asked for a bed for the night but was told that there was not one available and was advised to try at the White Hart, which stood almost opposite. King eventually left the Blue Boar in the company of a fellow labourer, Charles Merret, who offered to help him find accommodation. Unfortunately, all the pubs were closed and the two men ended up sleeping in a hay loft, close to the Bear Inn.

The Blue Boar, where King met with Charles Merret. (© N. Sly)

While coroner Mr Edward Coucher and magistrate Thomas Goodlake arrived at the White Hart to open the inquest, the police set off for the bean fields to talk to the two labourers, who were taken into custody and brought back to Wantage separately. When the two men were interviewed, it soon became evident that Merret had nothing whatsoever to do with the gruesome murder. He had already been drinking at the Blue Boar for some time when King came in and offered him a shilling to go home with him, which he had accepted. King, on the other hand, was giving the police the first of a number of conflicting statements about the murder.

When he was first apprehended, a search of his pockets revealed a purse, similar to that owned by Anne Pullen, and numerous silver coins, including the crooked sixpence that the deceased woman was known to carry with her for luck. There were also what looked like spots of fresh blood on his coat. Naturally, King had a ready explanation for the presence of the purse and sixpence and the bloodstains.

He first said that, on the night of the murder, he had been in the company of a man named Edward 'Ned' Grant from Hanney, who had called in at the White Hart for a pint of beer. According to King, he had been waiting outside for about five minutes when he heard the sound of a scuffle from within the pub. When he went inside to investigate, he saw the landlady lying decapitated in the kitchen, her blood spurting over the walls. Grant had quickly pushed him outside and handed him the dead woman's purse along with some loose coins, telling him that if he 'split' he would be killed himself the next time he and Grant met. Grant had then headed off alone towards the village of Sparsholt, leaving King frightened and distressed. He had gone to the Blue Boar Inn, where he had met Charles Merret and, fearful of being attacked by Grant, had given Merret a shilling to keep him company.

King was brought before the coroner and, having first been cautioned, proceeded to tell him in private that he knew the identity of the murderer, repeating his accusation against Ned Grant. Meanwhile, the police had begun an immediate search for Ned Grant but it quickly became apparent that no such person existed, other than in the imagination of George King.

Just as the inquest was about to close, King spoke out, telling the coroner that he could not be easy until he told the truth. Now he accused Charles Merret of committing the murder. Since the inquest had already heard sufficient evidence to exonerate Merret, the coroner's jury had no hesitation in returning a verdict of 'wilful murder' against George King.

As King was being transported to Reading Gaol he gave yet another account of the murder to his escort, PC James Jackson, which was probably the closest to the truth so far. Now King admitted that he alone had struck the fatal blow, which had so neatly decapitated Mrs Pullen. He told the police that he had gone into the pub in search of a bed for the night and that he had asked Mrs Pullen if he could possibly share her bed! Mrs Pullen had been both shocked and enraged and had threatened to knock his head off with a poker. King had defended himself with the reaper's sickle that he used in his work, intending only to hit the landlady over the head with the back of the sickle. However, to his dismay, the single blow had somehow swiped her head clean off her shoulders.

King admitted to ripping the pocket off Mrs Pullen's dress to steal her money, later discarding the pocket in a river. He also admitted to taking the keys to the inn, saying that he had lost them on his road home. (The track along which he walked to work the next day was subsequently searched and the keys found.)

Charged with the murder of Mrs Pullen, George King stood trial at the Lent Assizes in Reading on 28 February 1834, before Mr Justice Patteson. The case was prosecuted by Mr Curwood and Mr Jeffrey Williams, with Mr Carrington and Mr Stone acting in King's defence.

King was only a small man, standing just a fraction over 5ft 2in tall, yet his frame was described as 'strong and sinewy' and, according to the *Reading Mercury*, 'he must have possessed almost Herculean power.' The newspaper described his features as 'squat, sullen and forbidding; his cheekbones prominent, his eyes small and sunken, his forehead low and contracted and his ears protruding greatly from his head'. Although King pleaded not guilty to the murder of Mrs Pullen, his demeanour throughout his trial was sullen, apathetic and indifferent and he refused the chance to speak in his own defence.

In his summary of the evidence for the jury, the judge reminded them of the numerous different and often contradictory statements that the defendant had made, asking them to ascertain whether his most recent confession was corroborated by the evidence they had heard in court. The jury needed very little time to reach a conclusion and quickly pronounced King 'Guilty' of the wilful murder of Mrs Pullen.

Mr Justice Patteson passed sentence of death on George King, who learned without displaying even a flicker of emotion that he was to die on the scaffold in three days time, on his nineteenth birthday.

Shortly before his execution, King made yet another confession to the prison chaplain, in which he indicated that he had originally intended to rob Mrs Pullen but instead had impulsively killed her, almost on a whim, when the opportunity presented itself. This was consistent with the evidence of a post-mortem examination on Mrs Pullen's body, at which it was surmised that the attack on the dead woman had been made from behind, while she was seated, and had probably taken her completely by surprise. King added numerous details to his latest confession, including the fact that Mrs Pullen's body continued to move for some time after her head was cut off.

King was executed at Reading Gaol on 3 March 1834 before a large crowd of spectators, more than a third of whom were women. His death was not instantaneous and he continued to struggle and shudder violently for some time at the end of the rope before finally expiring. After hanging for the customary one hour, his body was cut down and, prior to his burial within the prison grounds, a plaster of Paris cast was taken of his face.

In order to facilitate the casting process, King's head was shaved, revealing an enormous skull fracture that was almost 5in long and three-quarters of an inch wide, which he had sustained some years earlier in a fall from a hay loft.

Mrs Pullen's murder is surely one of the most horrific in the annals of true crime and yet the actions of her killer, George King, who is variously described in the contemporary newspapers as 'a ferocious monster' and 'an inhuman beast', are almost eclipsed by the behaviour of the dead woman's relatives after her death. According to the *Reading Mercury* Mrs Pullen's family – including her own mother – were '…so utterly callous to all sense of decency, as on Sunday to make a sort of exhibition of the bloody kitchen and mangled body to all persons who were willing to drink a pint of beer as the price of admission, and on Monday after the close of the inquest, when the body had been placed in a coffin, numbers of persons were admitted on paying for the sight, the neck being left bare that all might see the horrible spectacle of the place where it had been severed from the body.'

Note: The murder of Anne Pullen has become something of a legend in the area around Wantage and, as with most long-running legends, facts occasionally become distorted. Thus there is an alternative account of the murder which places the scene of the crime at another Wantage pub, the Red Lion. Anne Pullen is described as a barmaid, who was too busy to serve George King immediately when he called for ale. In annoyance, he flung his money on the floor, decapitating Anne when she stooped to pick it up. I have taken my account from contemporary newspaper reports of the murder. There are, however, several discrepancies between different newspapers. Anne Pullen is alternatively named Pullin and Charles Merret is also referred to as Merriet, Marriet and Marriot.

5

'THAT SETTLED HER OFF AND ENTIRELY MURDERED HER'

Woodcote, 1839

Fanny Phillips was a widow, who lived alone in a cottage in the village of Woodcote. Having reached the age of eighty-four, she was becoming increasingly physically and mentally frail but, with the help of her neighbours, she was able to continue living in her own home. Every morning, Mrs Mary Lambden would visit Mrs Phillips's cottage and unlock the door. She would help the elderly lady to get up and dress herself then, each evening, she would help her back to bed. Mary Lambden kept the key to Mrs Phillips's cottage and would routinely lock the door at night, taking the key home with her.

On the morning of 8 May 1839, Mary Lambden arrived as usual to tend to her elderly neighbour. However, as she approached the cottage, she noticed that the door had been forced. Mrs Lambden immediately went home to fetch her husband, James, who returned to Mrs Phillips's home with her and went inside to investigate. He found Mrs Phillips lying dead in her bed, her bed linen soaked in the blood which had poured from terrible wounds in her head.

Local magistrate Adam Duff, who lived close to Fanny Phillips, was one of the first to respond to the Lambdens' calls for assistance and, as he approached her cottage, he spotted a small canvas bag on the doorstep. The bag contained a sawyer's measuring rule, a file without a handle, a line and reel and a compass. Duff passed the bag and its contents to the Henley police constable, Henry Stephens.

Stephens conducted a search of the cottage, noticing that the door appeared to have been prised open from the outside, probably using a bar of some kind. Mrs Phillips's house had been ransacked and whoever had attacked and robbed her had even forcibly removed her wedding ring, leaving a deep scratch on her ring finger.

The bag and its contents were soon traced to a sawyer named John Hore, from whom they had been stolen on 25 March. Hore was able to positively identify the bag as one belonging to him, which had disappeared from his place of work at College Wood. The contents of the bag had also once belonged to him, although he was unable to be absolutely certain about the file, since the handle had been removed since it was stolen.

As the police began their enquiries into the murder of Fanny Phillips, James Lambden recalled something unusual. Lambden worked on a farm at Woodcote and one of his colleagues was a man named Charles Morley. Morley had known that Mrs Lambden visited and cared for Fanny Phillips and, two weeks before the murder, Morley had been asking some searching questions.

He wanted to know whether anyone ever visited Mrs Phillips after Mary Lambden had locked up the cottage for the night. 'I wonder she's not afraid to live there by herself,' mused Morley. He had then wondered how Mrs Phillips was able to support herself, asking, 'Is she kept by the parish?' Lambden assured Morley that the widow had enough to live on, telling him, 'She is a stingy old creature and some people are apt to think she has some guineas left now.'

Lambden went on to tell the police that, only the day before the murder, the workers had been thirsty and someone had suggested buying beer. Morley said that he had no money to pay for beer, yet not long after the murder was discovered, Lambden had seen him coming out of a beer shop, obviously tipsy.

PC Stephens went to see the owner of the beer shop and asked him some questions about Morley's drinking habits. Richard Lewis told him that Morley had begun drinking at eight or nine o'clock in the morning and had been in and out of the beer shop all day, until late evening. Morley had paid for his beer with half a crown and Lewis had noticed that he had several shillings in his purse.

Stephens went in search of Morley and, when he located him, took him back to the cottage Morley shared with his wife and questioned him. Morley said nothing to incriminate himself in the murder of Fanny Phillips but when Stephens searched the cottage, he found another file hidden in the chimney corner. Morley denied ever having seen it before, suggesting that his wife may have put it there without his knowledge. Yet he quickly changed his story, telling PC Stephens that he had actually found the file lying on the roadside at Deadman's Lane. He even took the constable to point out exactly where he had found it.

Stephens showed the file to John Hore, who immediately identified it as one that had been in his tool bag when it was stolen. By now, Stephens was pretty sure that the thief was Charles Morley and he was also convinced that, if the file had once been in the bag that was found outside the dead woman's home, then it stood to reason that whoever had stolen the bag must be her killer. Yet a constable's gut instinct was not hard evidence and, apart from the tool bag and the fact that Morley had shown an unusual interest in the victim's habits prior to her untimely death, there was nothing whatsoever to link him with the murder.

The only offence that Morley could be charged with was the theft of the bag and the tools it contained. He was arrested and brought for trial and, because he had previous convictions, he was sentenced to transportation for seven years. He was taken from Oxford Gaol, where he had been imprisoned prior to his trial, to a prison hulk on the River Thames, to await his enforced passage to Australia.

While incarcerated, Morley shared a cell with Joseph Blackall, who was charged with sheep rustling and was awaiting his own trial. Blackall was eventually acquitted and, on his release, he approached the police with information he had learned from his cell mate.

Morley couldn't resist boasting that he had '...more money than any fellow who ever came into this house'. He asked Blackall if he knew the little house in Woodcote near Mr Duff's and, when Blackall said that he did, Morley told him, 'That was where the old woman lived that I have murdered.' He went on to explain that he had gone to the house thinking that Mrs Phillips had money concealed there and that she had risen up in bed and he believed she had recognised him. Afraid that she could identify him, he hit her three times over the head with a hammer. 'That settled her off and entirely murdered her,' he told Blackall, adding that Mrs Phillips had 'a rare swag' of money, which he had carried home and hidden in the thatched roof of his cottage. By the weight of the money bags, Morley believed that he had netted around £300 and he was now anxious that his wife should be made aware of the location of his haul so that she could retrieve some of the cash and use it to pay for his defence. If his wife didn't send the money, he intended to get out, go home and murder her.

With this new information, PC Stephens, the Nettlebed constable PC Giles and the Woodcote constable, William Ham, conducted a further search of Morley's cottage on 26 July. Leaving Giles and Stephens inside the building, Ham shinned up a ladder onto the roof and began to tear away the 8in thick thatch. Soon he had removed a complete section of the roof the size of an apron and, not only could he see his colleagues inside the cottage but also two bags which had obviously been concealed between the internal beams and the thatched roof. Although Morley's was just one of three homes under the same thatched roof, the separate dwellings were divided by wattle and daub walls and the position of the bags meant that they could only have been placed there from within Morley's cottage.

When the bags were emptied, one was found to contain 232 sovereigns and 10 half-sovereigns and the other 19 guineas and 10 half guineas, 2 half-sovereigns, a 7 shilling piece and an old silver coin.

Morley's brother-in-law, Henry Burgess, visited him on the prison hulk to tell him that the money had been found. Morley's first reaction was to ask Burgess exactly how much money had been recovered and, when Burgess told him, Morley insisted that they hadn't found it all. Burgess asked him what had happened to the old lady's wedding ring and Morley told him that it was in a razor case at his mother's home.

Burgess told Morley that he would surely be taken back to Oxfordshire and warned him against saying anything that might incriminate him, reminding him that it was his duty to protect his wife. Morley told Burgess that he should ask magistrate Adam Duff to take him back to Oxford as quickly as possible as he might 'do away with himself'.

Burgess relayed the conversation to Duff, who went to Morley's mother's home and found the wedding ring exactly where the prisoner had said it would be. With sufficient evidence against Morley, he was now officially charged with the murder of Fanny Phillips and stood trial at the Oxford Assizes on 2 March 1840 before Mr Justice Patteson. The case was prosecuted by Mr Maclean and Mr Phillimore, with Mr Rickards acting as defence counsel for the accused.

It was stated in court that thirty-four-year-old Morley had only confessed to his brother-in-law because he was under the impression that, having already been convicted of theft, he could not be tried for the murder of Mrs Phillips. Of course, he was very much mistaken. He was tried, found guilty and sentenced to death and, in spite of his protests of innocence, he was hanged at Oxford Gaol on 23 March 1840.

Note: Joseph Blackall is also named Joseph Blackhall in contemporary accounts of the murder.

6

'I'LL BE DAMNED IF I WON'T KILL HIM'

Broughton Castle, 1848

For many years, James Busby had held the position of gamekeeper to Lord Saye and Sele, the owner of Broughton Castle, near Banbury. In 1848, His Lordship did not actually live at the grand country house but rented it out to a tenant, Henry Corbet Wilson.

On 21 March 1848, a general sale of effects was advertised in the *Banbury Guardian*. Mr Wilson was about to leave the castle and had decided to sell some of his furniture and personal possessions. On 24 March, the day of the sale, Busby and the other members of staff were asked to make sure that everything ran as smoothly as possible and that no damage was done to the house and grounds by those attending.

It was a long and busy day for the staff and, at three o'clock in the afternoon, Mr Wilson instructed Busby and some of his colleagues to go to the Twistleton Arms public house to get some refreshments. (The inn has since been renamed the Saye and Sele Arms.) The workers took their dinner at the pub before returning to the castle.

It was almost eight o'clock in the evening by the time the sale had concluded and, once dismissed from his work, Busby went back to the pub with his son, George. The premises was crowded with drinkers, several of whom were James's colleagues or neighbours and James soon found a comfortable seat on a settle in the kitchen to drink his beer and chat.

However, the peace and conviviality of the evening was soon shattered by a local farmer, Richard Pargeter, who came into the pub and suddenly, without provocation, picked up an earthenware pint mug from a table and threw it straight at James Busby, the vessel striking him hard on the chest.

Broughton Castle, Banbury. (Author's collection)

Pargeter had been accompanied to the pub by a man named William Harris, who appeared both shocked and surprised by what his companion had just done. He seized Pargeter and remonstrated with him, 'You should not serve him so.'

'I'll be damned if I won't kill him,' replied Pargeter and began to struggle desperately against Harris's restraining clutches. The two men battled together for some time, Pargeter attempting to free himself so that he could fight James Busby and Harris trying equally hard to prevent him from doing so.

No words had passed between Pargeter and Busby, the latter of whom had made no attempt to retaliate but had instead stood up quietly, intending to leave the pub. As Harris and Pargeter grappled, they fell into the settle where Busby had been sitting moments earlier, enjoying a quiet beer. Once again, Busby attempted to leave the premises but now he had to squeeze past the two combatants and, as he did so, Pargeter lashed out at him, punching him in the face and then deliberately aiming a vicious kick at him, which connected with the lower part of Busby's belly.

Fortunately, Busby was still able to walk and left the pub in the company of his son, and a neighbour, Thomas Freeman. On his way home, Busby called at the home of County Magistrate Reverend C.F. Wyatt, presumably to make an official complaint about the assault. From there, the three men went to visit another neighbour, Mr Dyson, where they spent seven or eight minutes enjoying a pipe of tobacco before setting off to walk home to the village of North Newington, a distance of less than a mile from the Twistleton Arms.

By the time James Busby reached home, he was complaining of severe pain and was barely capable of walking. Having first put his father to bed, George carried on walking to Banbury, where he called at the home of surgeon Richard Grimbly to ask him to visit.

Grimbly arrived at about half past eleven that evening, finding James Busby in bed, complaining of being in great pain. Having examined Busby, Grimbly could see little signs of any serious injuries but applied leeches to the area and agreed to call again on the following morning. At his second visit, Grimbly realised that Busby had been hurt far more seriously than he had first thought. So serious was Busby's condition that Grimbly called in his partner, Mr Gibbs, for a second opinion.

By the time Gibbs and Grimbly examined James Busby later that afternoon, his condition was obviously extremely grave and, as a precaution, it was decided to take a deposition from him. The Reverend Wyatt was summoned to his bedside, and Busby dictated a statement, which he then signed.

He related how Pargeter had thrown the pint mug at him and detailed the resulting scuffle between Pargeter and Harris, as Harris tried his hardest to prevent Pargeter from striking him again. He told Wyatt that Pargeter had struck him in the face and then kicked him in the 'private parts', stating that he already had a hernia and was wearing his truss at the time of the attack on him. He described his walk home and his visit from the surgeon, saying:

> I have been in bed ever since and am now suffering most acutely. My sufferings are such that I don't think I can get better unless a great alteration takes place and I make this statement thinking that I am on my dying bed.

As soon as the deposition had been taken, a warrant was issued for the arrest of Richard Pargeter on a charge of assault. He was located at the Queen's Head pub in Banbury and, when the warrant was served on him by the Neithrop constable, Daniel Newton, Pargeter told him, 'This is all through that job that you took me to Oxford Gaol for.'

Newton recalled that ten years earlier Pargeter had been accused of poaching. He had been brought to trial and convicted, mainly because of evidence given against him in court by James Busby. Believing that he had been unfairly treated, Pargeter had held a grudge against Busby which had festered for ten years until he could contain it no longer.

Pargeter and Busby lived quite close together and had drunk in the same room of the same pub many times before in the years between Pargeter's conviction and the attack. Just why Pargeter's animosity towards Busby had finally come to a head on the previous evening was a complete mystery, although when arrested, Pargeter told the constable that he hoped he had killed Busby, adding, 'Then I shall be hanged and there will be an end of it.'

James Busby was sinking fast and, by seven o'clock on the evening of 25 March, he had lost his fight for life. Mr Grimbly conducted a post-mortem examination and found several patches of inflammation on Busby's bowels, along with 'a rupture of the coats of the small intestine called the ileum.' The rupture, which was about the size of a shilling piece, had caused the contents of Busby's gut to spill out into his abdomen, resulting in his death from peritonitis. Grimbly determined that the rupture had been caused by extreme violence to the abdomen, in the form of a kick or a blow.

Pargeter was brought before magistrates two days after the attack on Busby, the charge against him now upgraded from assault to wilful murder. After Busby's deposition was presented, a number of witnesses were called to give their account of the attack on him. These included George Busby, surgeon Richard Grimbly, PC Newton and a number of people who had been drinking in the Twistleton Arms at the time. Most testified to the fact that the attack on Busby had been completely unprovoked and that Pargeter had stated that, had he had a gun in his hand, he would have shot Busby. However, George Busby and William Harris, who had manfully restrained Richard Pargeter, both stated that James Busby had left the public house and then gone back in again.

Nevertheless, the magistrates – Colonel North, Reverend C.F. Wyatt and Reverend J. Ballard – felt that there was a case to answer against Pargeter and he was committed for trial at the next Oxford Assizes.

The trial opened on 18 July before Mr Justice Baron Rolfe, with Mr Keating appearing for the prosecution and Mr Pigot for the defence. However, now the evidence against Pargeter did not seem as clear cut as it had at the magistrates' court.

The pub had been very crowded and there was some confusion about just who had done what to whom and when. Most of the witnesses had heard Pargeter say that the quarrel between him and the victim was the consequence of the 'Oxford Gaol job' ten years earlier. Nearly all had heard Pargeter calling Busby a 'damned liar' and threatening to shoot him if he ever got the chance.

Everyone had seen Pargeter flinging the mug at Busby and some testified that they had witnessed Pargeter kicking the unfortunate victim in his 'private parts'. However, several witnesses came forward prepared to swear that Pargeter had not kicked Busby and that he was never actually close enough to the victim to land a kick.

Most witnesses said that Busby had quickly left the pub without any attempt at retaliation for the thrown beer mug but two witnesses swore that, having left, Busby then went back in, squared up to Pargeter and threatened to fight him, eventually having to be forcibly ejected from the inn. Everyone agreed that, although Pargeter appeared to have been drinking when he attacked Busby, he was not drunk.

Even the medical evidence was not as straightforward as it had first appeared, with Grimbly and Gibbs now disagreeing about Busby's injuries. Both surgeons were confident that the cause of Busby's death was peritonitis following a ruptured ileum and that the rupture might have been caused by a violent kick or blow, received when Busby was not expecting it. However, there were no external signs of any blow or kick and Busby himself had variously described the kick as having connected with his 'private parts' and also with his belly, just below his navel. Grimbly now told the court that Busby was wearing a steel truss at the time of the attack, even though there was no evidence that he suffered from a hernia. The truss itself was ancient – so old that the bindings on it had become as hard as the steel itself. The surgeons found themselves in disagreement about the exact location of the violent kick or blow, with one saying that it had landed above the truss and the other equally certain that the blow had landed on the truss itself and that the truss had been a contributory factor to the rupture of the ileum.

Mr Pigot, for the defence, told the jury that there was no evidence whatsoever of any murderous intent on the part of Pargeter against Busby, pointing out the fact that they had met numerous times since Pargeter's conviction for snaring animals with no show of violence between them. In fact, there was insufficient evidence to prove that Pargeter had even inflicted the injury that had caused Busby's death. Mr Pigot called two witnesses to attest to Pargeter's previous good character, both of whom swore that he was a sober, kindly and peaceable man.

With that impression fresh in the minds of the jury, the defence rested, leaving the judge to summarise the evidence. The jury then consulted for just ten minutes before returning with their verdict, pronouncing Richard Pargeter 'Not Guilty' of the wilful murder of James Busby but 'Guilty' of manslaughter, with a recommendation to mercy.

The judge approved the verdict, saying that he believed there were some mitigating circumstances. Because of these, he sentenced Richard Pargeter to imprisonment for just eight calendar months.

7

'SHE WAS AS COLD AS A CLOD'

Watlington, 1850

At eleven o'clock on the night of 25 September 1850, there was a knock on the door of labourer Moses Robinson's cottage in Watlington. When Moses answered it, he found his fifty-year-old neighbour, John Lambourn, on his doorstep. 'Will you come along with me, for I think my wife lies dead in the garden?' asked Lambourn politely.

Moses and his brother William followed Lambourn back to his cottage, where they found Ann Lambourn lying on her back, near the front door. Moses Robinson knelt and touched the woman and found that her heart was still beating very faintly. He called for a light and, when one was brought, he could see that Ann's cap was saturated in blood, which had pooled on the ground where she lay. She had no shoes on her feet and her hands were bloody, clenched tightly into fists and desperately clutching a few blades of grass.

Ann Lambourn was described as 'a poor little object'. Some years older than her husband, she was frail and emaciated and was also partially deaf. She was carried to her bed, with John Lambourn fussing around her, repeatedly saying, 'My poor old wife.' Lambourn said that someone must go for the doctor, to which Moses Robinson replied that he should go himself. Lambourn immediately set off to fetch a doctor but met baker, Samuel Lewis, and asked him to go instead, while he fetched his sister.

Surgeon Mr Dickson hurried to Ann's bedside, noting that she had numerous head wounds. In spite of her general frailty, Ann clung desperately to life, not succumbing to her injuries until twenty past eight the following morning.

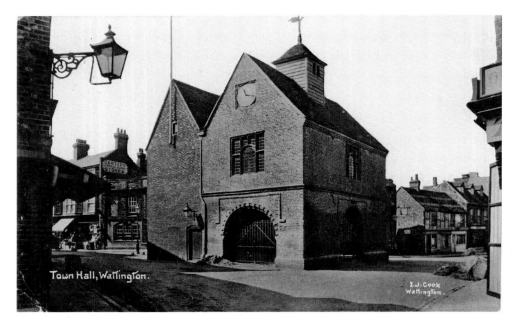

Watlington, 1900s. (Author's collection)

Dickson carried out a post-mortem examination and found that she had been struck on the right side of the back of her head, the resulting laceration going down to the bone, although her skull beneath wasn't fractured. There was a further wound on the back of her head and another on one cheek. The injuries had caused the formation of a blood clot at the base of her brain.

John Lambourn told the surgeon that he would find bruising on Ann's body as she had frequently 'thrown herself about'. Dickson did indeed find faint bruises all over Ann's pitifully thin body, although he did not think that they had contributed to her death, which he believed had been caused by blood loss, combined with the head wound and the blood clot. Dickson believed that Ann's injuries had been inflicted about an hour before he was summoned and that it was impossible that they could have resulted from a fall or a fit. He theorised that Ann had been violently struck, probably inside the cottage, and had then staggered out into the garden. In daylight, he was able to find a large quantity of blood all over the garden, which, in the words of the local newspaper, 'had spurted out as though from a waterspout'. Dickson believed that Ann had stumbled around the garden for some time, before collapsing exhausted in the doorway of the cottage, weak through loss of blood.

An inquest was opened on 30 September at the Hare and Hounds Inn in Watlington, by the North Oxfordshire coroner, Mr John Henry Cooke. From evidence heard at the inquest, it soon became apparent that the Lambourns' marriage was a far from happy one.

Neighbours spoke of countless violent arguments between the couple and of regular beatings meted out to Ann by her husband, either with his fists or with sticks. John Lambourn had been heard to threaten her life numerous times. Less than three weeks before her death, he had visited a pub in nearby Caxham and told everybody in the bar that if he could get rid of that 'old brute' of his, he could get a nice young woman. He had repeatedly wished his wife dead, with the daisies growing over her and, in front of witnesses, had often threatened to '...cut her dear old head off'. He had told several people that he would kill his wife and that, sooner or later, he would be hung for her.

One of the series of violent arguments had been just two days before Ann's death and had erupted after she had spent four shillings. Mrs Coles, who lived in the adjoining cottage with her husband, William, told the inquest that, whenever the Lambourns began one of their violent altercations, she would have to leave her own house. She couldn't bear to hear Ann being beaten and abused and yet couldn't bring herself to interfere.

Mr and Mrs Coles had last seen Ann Lambourn alive at about five o'clock in the afternoon of 25 September, when she had come round to their home for a light for her fire. At half past seven, Mr and Mrs Coles went out and they next passed the house an hour later, when they heard the Lambourns quarrelling, with John Lambourn shouting at his wife that she should have made the tea earlier. When they returned home at eleven o'clock, the door to the Lambourns' cottage was ajar, although there was no light within.

However, Mr and Mrs Coles didn't find this particularly unusual, since Mary Lambourn habitually sat in the dark at nights, waiting for her husband to come home from the pub. Soon after midnight, Mr and Mrs Coles were roused from their bed with news of the brutal attack on their neighbour.

The coroner's jury consulted for a short time before returning a verdict of 'wilful murder against John Lambourn'. He was immediately taken to Oxford Castle where he was imprisoned to await the next assizes.

His trial opened on 4 March 1851 before Mr Justice Patteson, with Mr Carrington and Mr Skinner prosecuting and Mr Williams appearing for the defence.

The court heard from many of the witnesses who had already spoken at the inquest, most of whom repeated their allegations of the beatings, threats and cruel words that Ann Lambourn had endured throughout her marriage. William Coles testified to the fact that John Lambourn had visited his home at about one o'clock in the morning, while Ann Lambourn's life was slowly ebbing away in the adjoining cottage. Lambourn had been concerned about how long his wife would survive and whether or not her death would 'demand a jury'.

Another villager, Samuel Gould, told the court that he had seen the body of Ann Lambourn after her death and had remarked to John that she was '...as unkind a sight as he had ever seen'. Lambourn replied that his wife must have been murdered by someone, insisting, 'I am innocent of it.'

Lambourn had told people that he had been out on 25 September and that when he came home, there had been no light in the house. He heard a gurgling noise outside and went to see what it was, finding his injured wife lying on the doorstep. However, Moses Robinson testified that Lambourn could not possibly have entered the house without seeing Ann.

Robinson related being called to the Lambourns' house by John. He had picked Ann up to carry her indoors and told the court, 'She was as cold as a clod,' adding that her clothes were quite damp.

Surgeon Mr Dickson described Ann's wounds and the conclusions he had drawn from the examination of her body and then dropped a bombshell – in the chimney corner of the Lambourns' cottage, a pair of fire tongs had been found on the morning of Ann's death and they were heavily stained with fresh blood, to which a few hairs adhered.

Things were looking decidedly black for John Lambourn until Mr Williams began to speak in his defence. Williams pointed out that Ann Lambourn's blood was 'scattered about in every direction' and that her bonnet was saturated with it. In spite of this, no blood had ever been found on any of John Lambourn's clothes. It was the contention of the defence that there was no evidence whatsoever to suggest that John Lambourn had murdered his wife. She could just as easily have been killed by a band of ruffians, bent on robbing the house, who were disturbed before they could actually steal anything.

Having summarised the evidence for the jury, Mr Justice Patteson left it to them to decide whether or not they believed that Ann Lambourn had been killed by her husband. The jury deliberated for an hour before returning to acquit John Lambourn of the charge of wilful murder against him. Nobody else was ever charged with the murder of the 'poor little object' that was Ann Lambourn and her murder remains unsolved.

Note: In some contemporary newspaper accounts of the murder, the Lambourns' name is alternatively spelled Lambourne. To confuse matters further, the names John and Ann Lamborn appear on official records, which seem to show that the couple were both fifty when Ann was killed, even though most of the newspapers describe her as older than her husband. There is also some discrepancy about the neighbours, the Robinsons. Some newspapers state that the cottage belonged to Moses Robinson and that he was visited by his brother, William, while others have William as the owner and Moses as the visitor. The surgeon is alternatively named Mr Dickson and Mr Dixon.

8

'UNCLE DEAD – THREE MEN'

Williamscot, 1852

[Note: The following is an account of the murder of an Italian man by his nephew. Since both the murderer and his victim are called Giovanni Kalabergo, the anglicised names they adopted while living near Banbury will be used to differentiate between them.]

Giovanni Kalabergo came to England from Italy to avoid being conscripted into Napoleon's army and by 1852 he had been settled in Banbury for more than forty years, even anglicising his name to John. A highly respected jeweller and maker of clocks, watches and barometers, Kalabergo had never married and had no relatives in England.

However, he did have a twenty-two-year-old nephew in Italy who was very keen to join him in Banbury. Giovanni Brazilli Guilielmo Kalabergo – also known as William – wrote to his uncle several times, telling him that it was his lifetime ambition to settle down in England. At first John was not interested in accommodating the young man, who was known in his native Italy as a bit of a troublemaker, but when William's father added his weight to his son's campaign of persuasion, John found it increasingly difficult to refuse. Eventually, he agreed that his nephew could come and live with him but he laid down very strict conditions for the young man's stay. William must behave like a real English gentleman and would be expected to be obedient at all times, attentive to his religious duties and avoid bad company.

When William arrived in England in October 1851, he found his uncle to be much stricter than he could ever have imagined. John seemed permanently cross and was always quick to accuse the young man of laziness or bad behaviour of one kind or another. William was scolded constantly, particularly at meal times and, although John threatened more than once to put him out on the streets, he refused to advance William the fare to return to Italy.

On 9 January 1852 the two men went out on John's cart, travelling from village to village selling watches and other small items. They were out all day and set off for home in the late evening. When they reached the steep Williamscot Hill, both men got out of the cart and walked, John leading the horse by its bridle and William following just behind the cart.

As they went up the hill, they were passed by Mr Walker, a baker from Banbury and, when Walker stopped his cart at a toll house, the Kalabergos' cart was not far behind him. Shortly afterwards, Walker heard the sound of two gunshots in quick succession that seemed to come from somewhere close by. The sudden noise startled Walker's horse and, when he had calmed the animal, he stood listening intently for a few minutes but, hearing no further sounds, he continued downhill on his way to Banbury. Meanwhile, there was yet another cart behind the Kalabergos' cart and, like John and William, the occupants dismounted to walk up the steep hill. They were led by a Mrs Saul from Thorpe Mandeville, who was walking a little ahead of the other passengers.

She had not walked far when she spotted what she thought was a greatcoat laying on the road. As she got nearer, she realised that it was in fact a man. Mrs Saul knelt and picked up the man's hand, which was still warm. Checking the man's wrist, Mrs Saul quickly realised that she could not feel a pulse and, looking round, she saw Kalabergo's driverless cart a little way ahead. By now, her companions had caught up with her and the man's body was loaded onto their cart and driven to a pub in Williamscot, while Mrs Saul followed on, driving the abandoned cart.

Back at the Kalabergos' residence, William had arrived home alone on foot in a state of near hysteria. Although he didn't yet speak much English, he shouted to the servants, 'Uncle dead! Uncle dead! Dead! Dead! Dead! Priest, priest.' Then, in an attempt to explain further he babbled, 'Uncle dead – three men!' He then performed an elaborate mime of striking someone with a stick and pointing the forefinger of his right hand, as if imitating a person shooting a gun.

John Kalabergo's servants sent for Catholic priest Dr William Tandy and a neighbour, Mr Bernhard Samuelson, who spoke a little Italian and was able to tease a more detailed account from the seemingly terrified young man. William related that he and his uncle had been travelling down the hill at Williamscot when three men had suddenly appeared out of nowhere and, after demanding money, shot John Kalabergo dead. William had run back up the hill as fast as he could, scrambling up a bank to get away from the bandits and losing his hat in the process. He then ran across the fields to his uncle's home to summon help, arriving between six and seven o'clock, breathless and in a state of great agitation.

Tandy escorted William to the police station and the two were taken back to the scene of the murder by police superintendent, Mr Thompson. On the way, they met

John Kalabergo's cart, which was being driven to his home. The cart still contained a number of valuable items, suggesting that robbery was not the motive for the fatal attack.

Several facets of William Kalabergo's account of John Kalabergo's murder did not ring true. He stated that he had run to his uncle's home to summon assistance, a journey that had taken him between seven and eight minutes. Yet, just a short while earlier, the Kalabergos had passed a toll house – if William had really been seeking help, why had he not returned there or even chased after Mr Walker's cart, which had passed him only a couple of minutes earlier?

William was detained under suspicion of the murder of his uncle while the police made further enquiries. He was kept under police guard in an attic room of the North Arms public house in Wroxton but, having complained that his handcuffs were too tight, he somehow managed to persuade his guards to unshackle him. Once free, he suddenly ran at the room's window, opened it and threw himself out. One of the policemen managed to snatch at his greatcoat as he slid down the thatched roof of the inn but the coat gave way, leaving William to plunge 32ft to the ground. Fortunately, Mrs Harris, the pub landlady, happened to glance out of the window and noticed William hobbling away towards the village. She alerted her husband who set off in hot pursuit and soon caught up with the fugitive – perhaps unsurprisingly, since he was later found to have broken bones in his right leg and left wrist and dislocated a bone in his foot.

North Arms public house, where William Kalabergo was held while under suspicion of his uncle's murder. (© N. Sly)

North Arms, Wroxton. (© N. Sly)

Meanwhile, the police had searched William's room at his uncle's house and found a loose bullet and gunpowder in the pocket of the young man's waistcoat. A post-mortem examination had been carried out on the victim by Dr Wise, at which it was noted that a bullet had entered his head by his right ear, passed through his brain and come to rest near his left ear. There was no indication that John Kalabergo had been beaten. The bullet retrieved from his brain was identical to those found in William's room. A wider search of the premises revealed a bullet mould hidden under the slate roof of the stable, along with a pistol bag and more powder and bullets, one of which was made from lead, others of which were made from a whitish metal. The police traced the purchase of a gun, bullet mould and powder to a Banbury gunsmith, Thomas Watkins.

When interviewed, Watkins told the police that he had sold all the items to William Kalabergo on 15 December 1851. Kalabergo had asked to be shown how to use the mould to make bullets and Watkins had demonstrated with a piece of lead. Kalabergo took the lead bullet away with him and was thought to have melted down old Britannia metal spoons and teapots to make more bullets. John was known to have taken a job lot of old teapots in payment of a debt and, after his death, they were nowhere to be found. Also missing were two gold watches, which the servants told the police had been recently stolen from their master. He had noticed their loss on 16 December, the day after his nephew had purchased the pistol.

An inquest was opened at the Crown Inn, Williamscot, at which the coroner's jury returned a verdict of 'wilful murder' against William Kalabergo. On 13 January, a heavily bandaged William appeared before magistrates at the White Lion Hotel in Banbury, charged with his uncle's death. 'No, Sir. My innocence will appear,' insisted William in his broken English.

He pleaded 'Not Guilty' to the charge against him. Through his interpreter, Mr Samuelson, he explained that, on the night of the murder, three men had approached him and his uncle as they led their horse and cart down the hill and demanded, 'Your purse or your life'. According to his nephew, John Kalabergo had tried to defend himself, at which the second man pulled out a pistol and shot him twice.

Frightened, William had run away, hotly pursued by the third man of the group. When he had shaken off his pursuer, William said he had tried to stop a cart to get help for his uncle but hadn't been able to make the driver understand him. (A witness actually came forward to say that he had been flagged down by Kalabergo on the night of the murder but that the young man had been sobbing so much that he couldn't understand what he wanted.) William also stated that a man on horseback had wished him 'Good night' and again, a witness came forward to say that he had been that man.

William admitted to buying a pistol from Mr Watkins, saying that it had been bought on behalf of his uncle who had not been happy with it and had subsequently returned it.

The magistrates were not swayed by William's explanations and he was committed for trial at the next Oxford Assizes. When the proceedings opened on Tuesday 2 March, an appeal was immediately made to the presiding judge, Mr Justice Wightman, to defer the trial until the next assizes. The counsel for the defence, Mr Piggott, told the judge that his client was a stranger to the country and did not speak English very well. His brother-in-law was a notary, who lived in Italy and had been summoned to England to help with the trial. Although he had not yet arrived in the country, he was expected any day. Piggott also pointed out the negative press coverage of the murder in the local papers, saying that he believed that it was prejudicial and meant that his client was unlikely to get a fair trial.

Mr Justice Wightman considered the request until the following morning before turning it down. Saying that he was sure that impartial jurors could be found and that Kalabergo's brother-in-law was unlikely to be able to assist him, the judge decreed that the trial would go ahead as planned. An interpreter would be provided to ensure that the defendant fully understood his appearance in court.

Fair trial or not, the fact that John Kalabergo had not been robbed made his nephew the only viable suspect of his murder – who else would have had the motive, means and opportunity to kill him? William's conviction and subsequent death sentence were almost a foregone conclusion, in spite of the best efforts of his defence counsel, whose fees were paid from the inheritance that William had received on his uncle's death.

Shortly before his execution, William made a full confession to Dr Tandy, saying that John Kalabergo had been so strict with him that he had begun to rue the day he ever came to England. 'The Devil put it into his head...' that by killing his uncle, he would not only free himself from his control but would also gain an inheritance, being his uncle's sole heir. According to William, John was so severe and humiliating towards him that to make the slightest deviation from his rules was to risk being turned out of the house and left penniless and destitute on the streets of Banbury. Alone in a foreign country, with no friends or relatives and no means of paying for his return to his homeland, William found himself plunging into a 'deep melancholy' and losing his religious faith.

William admitted to stealing money from the till in his uncle's shop and using it to buy the pistol. He also confessed to the theft of the two gold watches, along with some silver watches, silver spoons and other trinkets, which he had hidden in a newly-dug grave in the Catholic church at Banbury. He had committed the murder alone, creeping up behind his victim as they walked down Williamscot Hill, placing the pistol behind his ear and pulling the trigger. John Kalabergo had fallen instantly, without ever knowing who had shot him.

William had fled across the fields, discarding his greatcoat and the pistol in a ditch as he ran. 'I had scarcely committed the crime when I repented of it,' William said, telling the priest that, even if his crime had remained undetected, he would have lived a life of misery and his very soul would have been lost.

Expressing regret for the disgrace and distress he had brought to his country, to England and to the inhabitants of Banbury, Kalabergo stated that his only concerns were that his uncle's soul may be lost eternally and the grief that his execution would cause his poor mother in Italy.

Once in the condemned cell at Oxford Gaol, Kalabergo made another unsuccessful attempt to escape, forcing the prison guards to keep him permanently in leg irons as he awaited his execution. However, he was unable to escape his date with the hangman at Oxford Gaol on 22 March 1852. Watched by a crowd of 10,000 people, twenty-two-year-old William Kalabergo stood on the scaffold apparently deep in prayer, before the trapdoor dropped beneath him and he fell instantly to his death.

Note: As might be expected, the contemporary newspapers of the time struggle with the spelling of the foreign names. There are several variations in spelling of the men's forenames and Kalabergo is alternatively spelled Kalabargo and even Haldbergo. As always, I have used the most common spelling for this account.

9

'I COULD NOT HAVE DONE IT UNLESS I HAD HAD SOME DRINK'

Upper Heyford, 1863

By 1863, Noah Austin had been courting mill owner's daughter Elizabeth Allen for several years and, although no date had been set, it was widely assumed that they would eventually marry. Many fathers would have viewed Austin as an ideal husband for his daughter. He came from a very respectable family, his father being a Wesleyan preacher, and had a thriving business as a butcher in the town of Heyford. However, there was something about Austin that Elizabeth's father, James, just did not like. James was perfectly happy for Austin to be a tenant in one of his properties but would rather that he didn't marry his daughter. The true cause of the animosity between Allen and Austin is not recorded and there was apparently no real argument or quarrel between them, although Austin appears to have been quite a volatile young man who had recently been bound over by magistrates to keep the peace, having threatened to shoot his father.

On 12 February 1863, both Allen and Austin went to Bicester market, Allen driving there alone and Austin going with his father in his gig, which they parked for the day at the Cross Keys Inn. During the course of the day, Austin and Allen met and Austin asked Allen for a lift home on his cart. He agreed and Noah went back to the Cross Keys to leave a message for his father with the ostler.

James Allen had left his cart at the White Hart Inn and waitress Eliza Baughan saw the two men going off together at the end of the day. At about ten minutes to six in the evening, the cart pulled in to the Jersey Arms at Middleton and both men alighted. Each had three pennyworth of brandy before continuing on their homeward journey, having stayed at the inn for no more than five minutes. They were later to call briefly at the home of Richard Maycock in Caulcott, although that time, Austin remained in the cart.

Forty minutes later, Noah Austin alone arrived on foot at Mr Allen's mill at Upper Heyford. Seeking out the miller, John Wooloff, he told him that Allen wanted him to meet him on the Caulcott road. According to Austin, they had been nearing home when two men hailed James Allen, asking to pay him for some barley meal and Allen had asked him to run to the mill to ask Wooloff to take the invoice to him.

Wooloff set off in the dark along the Caulcott road, soon finding his master's horse and trap in a gateway, the horse's reins secured around the top spar of the gate. However, there was no sign of James Allen. Raising his lantern, Wooloff searched the immediate area and, some 16 yards beyond the cart, he spotted something. It was James Allen and he appeared to be at least unconscious, if not dead.

Unable to rouse his master, the miller ran to the nearest cottage and its occupant, James Justice, found a lantern and hastened back to where Allen lay on the left-hand side of the road. With more light available the two men were able to see that Allen was lying dead on his back in a large pool of blood, a huge hole in the left side of his face. Asking Justice to stay with Allen, Wooloff ran to the home of Edward Berry at Upper Heyford for assistance. Berry went with him to the scene

Upper Heyford. (© N. Sly)

of what now appeared to be a shooting and, while Wooloff and Justice held up their lanterns, he went through the dead man's pockets.

The left-hand trouser pocket had been turned out and the right-hand pocket was unbuttoned. Both were empty. In the breast pocket of Allen's coat were a pocket book and a cheque and in his waistcoat pocket were twelve halfpenny coins. Allen's singed hat was found a few feet from his body.

The three men lifted Allen into the back of his cart, noting as they did the presence of several bloodstains on some sacks that were already there. Once the body had been taken back to Upper Heyford, surgeon John Person-Cresswell was summoned, finding the dead man to have a large wound on his face. Two days later, the surgeon performed a post-mortem examination with the assistance of Deddington surgeon Mr E.W. Turner.

The surgeons noted two wounds, the facial injury and a second wound on the back of Allen's head, which had completely shattered his skull, exposing the brain matter beneath. Both injuries appeared to have been caused by a pistol shot and two bullets were recovered from the dead man's brain. Either wound was judged to be sufficiently serious to cause death.

As the last person known to have seen James Allen alive, Noah Austin's account of events was obviously of great interest to the police. Having summoned John Wooloff to meet Allen, Austin had gone to Allen's home to see Elizabeth and had then gone to his own home. He was eating his tea when the news was broken to him that Mr Allen had been found murdered and immediately responded, 'Oh, is he? I am very sorry. I rode home with him from Bicester.'

An inquest was opened by Mr Churchill, the coroner for North Oxfordshire, at the National School Room in Upper Heyford. Noah Austin was called to give evidence and, having first been cautioned by the coroner, related that he and Allen had been driving home together when they were stopped within 300 yards of Heyford by two men who wanted to settle an outstanding account. At Allen's request, Austin had cut across the fields to the mill to ask John Wooloff to meet him with the bill.

The coroner called just one more witness before adjourning the inquest. A boy called George Buckle had been walking from Heyford at around the time of the murder and had heard a shot fired, followed about half a minute later by a second. Buckle walked a further 200 yards before meeting Noah Austin, who was running towards Heyford.

With the evidence that shots had been fired before Noah Austin reached the mill at Heyford, Chief Constable Captain Charles Mostyn-Owen questioned him further and, although Austin stuck to his story, he was arrested and charged with the wilful murder of fifty-six-year-old James Allen. Protesting his innocence, Austin asked if he was to be taken to Oxford. Told that he was he begged to be allowed to go and pay for a pig first, telling the policeman that the money was in his cash box and that Elizabeth Allen had the key. Mostyn-Owen did not allow him to go, instead taking him to Oxford Castle and asking Superintendent Moulden to retrieve the key.

When the key had been collected from Elizabeth Allen, Moulden and Superintendent Whadcoate went with PC John James to search Austin's home and outbuildings. The cash box yielded a canvas purse containing £10 in gold and 17s in silver. Beneath the purse was found a small key and a powder flask, bullet mould and twelve bullets, which were wrapped in a piece of the *Banbury Herald* newspaper. In a gig in Austin's yard, PC James found a six-barrel pistol and six caps, which were wrapped in a piece of the same newspaper as the bullets. Three of the pistol barrels had recently been fired. Elizabeth Allen identified the purse as belonging to her father, pointing out the initials J.A. on it, which she had marked herself. She told the police that her father had taken it with him on his trip to Bicester market and that it usually contained a small key, such as the one found in Austin's cash box.

As the police continued their enquiries in the area, more witnesses came forward with accounts of the evening of 12 February, including labourer John Hudson who had seen Allen's cart parked outside Mr Maycock's house. Hudson, who was walking home, had left the road to take a route that ran across fields. He had heard the cart travelling along the road, then heard two gun shots, after which the movement of the cart stopped. He described the location of the cart as next to Mr Creek's field – exactly where it had been found by John Wooloff after the murder.

The adjourned inquest was resumed on 19 February and, having heard all the evidence, the coroner's jury retired for a short period before their foreman, Mr Edmund Creek, told the coroner that it was his painful duty on behalf of his fellow jury-men, to record a verdict of wilful murder against Noah Austin.

By the time the case was heard by the local magistrates, the police had spoken to John Castle, a gunsmith from Bicester, who testified to having sold caps and powder to Noah Austin two days before the murder. The gun itself was purchased from gunsmith Mr Thomas Juliens Watkins of Banbury, apparently on the same day. Castle stated that Austin had told him that he needed a gun for protection, having recently been robbed of all his money at nearby Ardley Plantation. Austin, who was still insisting that he was not guilty, told the magistrates that he had mentioned the robbery at the time to the landlady of the public house at Stoke.

The chairman of the magistrates informed Austin that he would have every opportunity of bringing forward any evidence in his defence at his trial at Oxford Assizes. The trial opened on 5 March before Mr Justice Crompton, and the jury were quick to find Austin guilty as charged, leaving Crompton to pronounce the mandatory sentence of death.

From the condemned cell at Oxford Castle, Noah Austin was later to make a confession of sorts to Reverend Philip Wynter D.D. He assured Wynter that he had not purchased the pistol with the intent of shooting Mr Allen. However, on the day before the murder, Allen had 'behaved ill' towards Elizabeth, putting her out of the house. According to Austin, Elizabeth had told him, 'I wish some accident would happen to him.'

'I will see, but we shall be found out,' responded Austin, to which Elizabeth had reassured him that they wouldn't and asked him to visit her that evening to arrange it.

Austin had been at Allen's home, when Allen had returned very tipsy. Anxious to avoid an argument, Austin had left the mill in the belief that Elizabeth wanted her father dead.

In shooting James Allen, he believed that he was carrying out her wishes. Austin told the clergyman that he had taken Allen's purse to make it appear as though the motive for his murder was robbery. 'I could not have done it unless I had had some drink,' he said, telling the Reverend Wynter that he had gone to an inn in Bicester and drunk two pints of strong ale before going home with Allen. Austin ended his confession by saying that he had made this statement to ease the mind of his own poor afflicted father, to whom he had caused so much sorrow, and in the hope that doing so would bring about forgiveness from God. (Regardless of Austin's guilt or innocence, James Allen was known in the area as a man who was frequently intoxicated, described by some as 'a thorough soak'.)

Twenty-six year-old Noah Austin was hanged on 24 March 1863, in what was to be the last public hanging at Oxford Prison. Austin remained calm right up until the moment that hangman William Calcraft approached him, when he burst into tears. His legs gave way completely and he had to be held upright while his legs were strapped and the noose adjusted around his neck.

Shortly after his execution, the *Oxford Journal* printed what amounted to a denial of any implication of Elizabeth Allen's complicity in her father's murder, as outlined in Noah Austin's confession. The newspaper assured its readership that Mr Allen was a kind father and had never once turned his daughter out of the house. It also stated that, on the evening before the murder, rather than coming home tipsy, James Allen returned home early, ate two eggs for his supper and retired to bed at eight o'clock.

However, the newspaper then printed several extracts from letters written to Elizabeth by Noah during his incarceration with the comment, 'The following letters written by Austin to Miss Allen do not read like those of a criminal goaded into perpetrating a fearful murder by female influence.'

The first letter, dated 22 February, read:

Dear Elizabeth, I want to tell you several things: do come and see me. I pray the Lord may be on my side for he knows that I am innocent. I wish you knew as well as me that I did not do the deed for which I am committed. I do like you as well as I ever did – if we are absent in body, we are present in mind. You know, my dear, that I was out some nights and I had money with me on Thursday evening. I had about £12 with me. I bought the pistol to guard myself. I was stopped one night coming home again from Ardley Plantation. I never told you about it, because I knew it would fidget you and also our people at home – you know how they are. I can tell you about the purse if you will come. I say again, do come. I remain with my best love to you NOAH AUSTIN.

Five days later, Austin wrote:

> I am here for nothing: it is such a hard case when I am innocent. It is all stuff what that old chief told you.

Finally, after his trial, Austin wrote:

> My dear friend. You may rest assured that you can see me on Wednesday, if you will have the kindness to come and see me. I am sure that you must think about me – such a friend and true friend that I have been to you for nearly seven years. If you will come and see me I die happy; but if you won't it will be hard work. Dear friend, if I should not see you any more this side of eternity, I wish you every happiness you need both in body and in soul. I want to have a word or two with you and a parting blessing – let us part in love and peace, and no malice one towards the other. I have not the least spite towards you and I hope you have none to me – if we don't forgive, how shall we expect to be forgiven? With my best respects to you and love from your true friend, NOAH AUSTIN.

The newspaper added that the public could compare these letters with the confession and draw their own inferences.

10

'I HAVE HEARD HER THREATEN TO KILL THE CHILDREN HUNDREDS OF TIMES'

Tetsworth, 1869

At about half past ten on the morning of Tuesday 9 November 1869, two very frightened little girls from the Hyde family of Tetsworth appeared unexpectedly on the doorstep of Mrs Jane White. Both children were crying bitterly and, when Mrs White asked them whatever the matter was, they told her between sobs that their mother had sent them to her house and told them to stay there for an hour. Their mother and father had been arguing and fighting all night, said the girls, and their father had accused their mother of going with other men.

The distressed children went on to say that their father had left the house about an hour earlier and their mother had then sent them away, telling them to stay with Mrs White. However, she wouldn't let their brother, George, and sister, Henrietta, go too, insisting that they remain in the house with her. No sooner had the girls finished relating their story then Henrietta raced into the house, screaming hysterically that her mother had just murdered George.

Mrs White set off to investigate, calling first at the village grocer's shop to ask Mr Latham if he had heard anything amiss at the Hydes' home, as someone had told her that Mrs Hyde had killed her child. Latham told her that he had heard nothing untoward, so Mrs White went to check for herself.

When she opened the door of the Hydes' cottage, she was confronted by the dreadful spectacle of three-year-old George lying dead in a pool of blood on the floor, a deep cut across his throat almost severing his head from his body. Nearby, his thirty-eight-year-old mother sat in a chair, black in the face and gasping for breath due to a thin cord wound tightly around her throat.

Mrs White rushed to the doorstep and screamed for Mr Latham, who came running. Latham quickly cut the piece of string around Susannah Hyde's throat with his knife and her breathing gradually returned to normal. Once she was able to speak again, Susannah told Mrs White that she had killed George and that she had meant to kill Henrietta too but the girl had managed to escape. Having cut George's throat, Susannah had then attempted to commit suicide by cutting her own but had managed to make only four small nicks in the flesh before losing her nerve. Hence, she had then tried to hang herself with string, which had given way and left her nearly strangled. Furthermore, Susannah told Mrs White that she had fully intended to kill all her children on the previous weekend.

However, the children had been particularly affectionate towards her, especially George, who had 'fondled round her' and she had been unable to bring herself to kill him.

An inquest into George's death was opened that same evening before the coroner for South Oxfordshire, Mr H. Dixon. The inquest heard that Susannah Hyde was known as an industrious woman whose husband frequently deserted her, sending her no money and leaving her no means of supporting herself and their children. She had taken in sewing in order to earn enough to keep her family together – however, her husband was of the opinion that she had only managed to survive by selling her body to whoever would pay money to sleep with her. The coroner pointed out that there was absolutely no evidence whatsoever to support Edward Hyde's allegations of marital infidelity against his wife and neither was there anything to suggest that she had ever lived as a prostitute.

On the night before George's murder, Edward Hyde, a shoemaker, returned to his home after a period of absence. He and his wife had spent the entire night arguing and Edward told the inquest, 'I charged her with going with another man and believe I had just grounds for such a charge.' Edward continued to say that he had left the family home again at between nine and ten o'clock on the morning of the murder, at which time his wife and children were all well. Saying that his wife had a violent temper, Edward stated, 'I have heard her threaten to kill the children hundreds of times.' However, he did not consider that there was anything the matter with his wife's mind, when she didn't 'put herself in a rage'. He had not noticed any changes in her behaviour recently.

In fact nobody had noticed anything unusual about Susannah Hyde's behaviour prior to the murder of little George. Dr H.G. Lee of Thame was called to the scene of the murder and told the inquest that he had found George dead, the wound in his throat so serious that the doctor believed that it would have caused his death immediately it was inflicted due to massive blood loss. An open cut-throat razor was found close to George's body. It was produced at the inquest for the coroner's jury to examine, still bearing smears of the child's blood.

Dr Lee told the inquest that he had recently been treating Mrs Hyde's brother for a lengthy illness and had made her acquaintance then. He had never noticed anything even slightly peculiar about either her appearance or her behaviour. Shopkeeper Thomas Latham agreed, saying that he had known Mrs Hyde for a long time and had never noticed her to be any different from any of the other women in the village.

PC Henry Shatlock had been called to the murder scene and had arrested Mrs Hyde and charged her with the wilful murder of her son. Susannah had readily admitted to killing the boy and told Shatlock of her intention to kill all of the children on the previous weekend, had her heart not failed her in the face of their affectionate behaviour towards her. Shatlock had been walking his beat in Tetsworth at half past eleven on the night before the murder and his attention had been attracted by the sound of a violent argument coming from within the Hydes' cottage.

Shatlock stopped and listened to the argument, telling the inquest that he had immediately realised that Edward Hyde was intoxicated at the time. Edward was widely known in the village to be 'addicted to intemperance'.

The police officer had heard Susannah shouting at him, saying, 'You know the last time you went away you left me destitute. When you go away and come home again, you wonder how I get my living. I say it is by my own industry, with my needle. You can't call it living, it is starvation.'

Although she wasn't called to give evidence at the inquest, it emerged that Henrietta had been shut in another room of the cottage by her mother. Through a crack in the door, the terrified five-year-old had watched her mother kill her brother and then attempt to commit suicide. Henrietta had escaped from the room and had run to the closed front door, where she had managed to lift the latch using a poker, before fleeing to the safety of Mrs White's house for assistance.

Once all the evidence had been heard, the coroner turned to his jury and addressed them. 'Gentlemen, you have laboured hard to find out extenuating circumstances in the woman's favour but the case is only before you in the broad light of wilful murder.' The jury returned a verdict of 'wilful murder' against Susannah Hyde, who appeared before magistrates on that charge the following morning and was committed to stand trial at the next Oxford Assizes.

Susannah Hyde's trial opened before Mr Baron Martin on 3 March 1870, with Mr Druce appearing for the prosecution. Susannah was not defended and immediately confounded the court by determinedly pleading 'Guilty' to the charge against her of the wilful murder of George Hyde.

Mr Baron Martin could do nothing but don the black cap and pass the mandatory death sentence. However, having done so, he addressed Susannah Hyde, telling her that, after reading the depositions, he did not have the slightest doubt that a jury would have found her guilty as charged, otherwise he would have tried to persuade her to change her plea to the more customary one of 'Not Guilty'. His Lordship stated that he had passed sentence of death only because the

Holloway Castle Prison, one of the gaols where Susannah Hyde was incarcerated in the 1800s. (Author's collection)

law of the land obliged him to do so. However, he fully intended to confer with the Secretary of State and endeavour to get that sentence commuted.

The judge was as good as his word and the Secretary of State announced soon afterwards that he had reduced Susannah Hyde's sentence to one of penal servitude. From Oxford Prison, she was sent to Holloway Prison, after which she was transferred to the Female Convict Prison at Knaphill in Woking. By 1881, she was still an inmate there, now aged fifty-six years old. Meanwhile, Henrietta, aged five, having witnessed her younger brother's gruesome murder, was sent to live with an aunt and uncle at Haddenham in Buckinghamshire. She later appears aged seventeen in the records of the workhouse at Thame, where she is described with the single word 'Lunatic'.

11

'I DON'T CARE WHAT BECOMES OF MY SOUL'

Witney, 1871

Thirty-six-year-old Edward Roberts was a man who could turn his hand to almost anything. Known in his native Witney as an honest and industrious man, he had worked as a farm labourer, gardener and carpenter. Yet his reputation and good character were entirely dependent on his ability to stay sober. Having once been a teetotaller, a job in a brewery at Islip introduced him to the pleasures of drink and, from then on, he developed a fondness for alcohol that soon led to him being sacked for habitual drunkenness. He was prone to frequent periods of binge drinking, some lasting for a week or more and, under the influence of drink he became violent, aggressive and foul mouthed.

Roberts lodged with Mrs Hester Merrick in Meeting House Lane in Witney and, in the eighteen months in which he lived there, he developed a crush on Mrs Merrick's daughter, Ann. However, Ann did not return his affections and Roberts found himself tortured by living in such close proximity to the love of his life. He constantly tried to persuade Ann to accept him as a husband and, on 28 May 1871, Edward and Ann quarrelled about his persistent and unwanted attempts to woo her, the exchange ending with Ann telling her devastated would-be suitor that she was actually courting a man from Oxford.

From that moment on, Ann tried to ignore Edward, which was not easy considering that they lived under the same roof. Edward grew more and more frustrated and lovesick and, by 29 July, his emotions had reached fever pitch.

On that day, he met Mrs Celia Lambourne who lived next door to the Merricks. 'Come and drink with me,' he told her. 'It will be the last time.' Mrs Lambourne went

Witney, Edward Roberts's home town. (Author's collection)

with Roberts to The Marlborough public house in the town and both drank a pint of beer. 'I shall kill Ann Merrick tonight or tomorrow morning,' Roberts told her casually as they sat with their drinks.

'Don't for heaven's sake talk about doing such a thing as that, Ned,' cried the horrified Mrs Lambourne. 'Think of your soul and Ann's too. What's to become of them?'

'I don't care what becomes of my soul,' replied Roberts. 'Hell's my portion and as for my body, you can go and bury it under the Butter Cross. I shall have Ann's head and the other bugger might have her body.'

Mrs Lambourne stayed at the pub drinking with Roberts, mulling over what he had said and, by the time she left the pub, was sufficiently convinced of his violent intentions towards Ann to go straight to the Merricks' house to warn her. Ann, however, did not seem overly concerned.

Roberts returned to his lodgings later that evening and, having watched him staggering drunkenly home, Mrs Lambourne could hear him cursing and shouting through the adjoining wall. She went next door to see if everything was all right and found Roberts slouched in a chair, a jug and glasses on a nearby table. He continued carousing noisily until well after midnight, at which time he quietened down enough for Mrs Lambourne to get some sleep.

The next morning, when Mrs Merrick left the house to go to church, Edward Roberts was drinking a cup of tea, while Ann was busy doing housework. By half past eleven, Roberts was sitting by the fire smoking his pipe, where he was eventually joined by the other lodger at the house, an elderly man named John Godfrey. Ann, meanwhile, had fetched a bucket of water and a cloth and was on all fours, washing the floor.

Without saying a word, Roberts suddenly got up and left the room, returning moments later with something held behind his back. Godfrey could hardly believe his eyes as Roberts marched up to Ann and raised both hands over his head. Only then did Godfrey realise that Roberts was holding an axe and, before Godfrey could intervene, Roberts swung the axe swiftly downwards, striking Ann Merrick a devastating blow on her head. He then calmly replaced the axe in the back kitchen where it belonged, walked back past the dumbstruck Godfrey and continued out through the front door.

Ann Merrick lay senseless on the floor, the axe blow having taken a complete slice of scalp, skull and brain off the back of her head. Godfrey rushed out of the house in search of help, grabbing the first passer-by he encountered and gabbling so fantastic a story that the startled man, Howell Ball, could scarcely believe what he was hearing. Having first rushed into the house to observe the carnage for himself, Ball set off up the street in pursuit of Edward Roberts and soon caught him up.

Roberts was strolling along, seemingly without a care in the world, still puffing away at his pipe. 'Oh, Ned, what have you been doing?' Ball asked him, to which Roberts replied that Ann had 'served him bad' and that he hoped that she was dead. He indicated to Ball that he was heading for the police station to turn himself in. Ball accompanied him for a few minutes then, spotting the local police officer, Superintendent Cope, Ball hailed him and suggested that he placed Roberts under arrest for murder.

Cope was incredulous, scarcely able to comprehend the thought that so brutal an act had occurred in the normally quiet and peaceful town. He grasped Roberts by the arm and announced his intention of taking him back to the Merricks' house to see what had happened there. Roberts had no intention of going anywhere of the sort. 'No, don't take me down there,' he pleaded, 'I don't want to see her any more. It's all right, I've done it. I hope her soul is in Heaven.'

Cope escorted Roberts to the cells at the town police station before heading back to Meeting House Lane, where a large crowd had gathered. Ann Merrick was being attended to by a doctor, so the police officer returned to the station, where he charged Roberts with assault with intent to murder. Cope noted that his prisoner was still under the effects of the alcohol he had consumed the previous night but, even so, Roberts freely admitted to striking Ann with the axe, making a statement in which he insisted that jealousy had been the cause of the attack and that he loved Ann as much as he loved his own life.

In spite of the seriousness of her injuries, Ann Merrick lingered until 25 August, at which time the charge against Roberts was elevated to one of wilful murder. Roberts was committed for trial at the next Oxford Assizes, which opened before Mr Justice Byles on 2 March 1872. The case was prosecuted by Mr Sawyer, while, at the request of the judge, Mr Pritchard undertook Roberts's defence.

The fact that Edward Roberts had struck the axe blow that killed Ann Merrick was not under dispute. However, his defence counsel contended that, in order to satisfy the charge of murder, Roberts had to have been capable of forming a clear and definite intention at the time the blow was inflicted, either to cause grievous bodily harm, maim or kill. Given that Roberts had been intoxicated, his condition not only rendered him liable to act on instinctive impulse but also made him completely incapable of forming any such clear and distinct intention in his mind. Whereas drunkenness was not a valid excuse for the crime and his client couldn't reasonably expect to be acquitted, Mr Pritchard insisted that the proper verdict was one of 'guilty of manslaughter' rather than 'guilty of wilful murder'.

In his summary of the evidence for the jury, Mr Justice Byles effectively ruled out the option of manslaughter, instructing them that drunkenness was no excuse for the crime. If it were, then a man might escape the consequences of his act simply by voluntarily making himself drunk. Thus, the only real concern for the jury was determining whether or not the accused actually committed the act with which he was charged. The jury deliberated for barely three minutes before finding Roberts 'Guilty' of the wilful murder of Ann Merrick.

He was hanged by William Calcraft at Oxford Prison on 19 March 1872. It was the first private execution to be held at the prison, observed only by selected members of the press, who joined the usual formal witnesses by invitation.

12

'THE VERY DEVIL TEMPTED ME TO DO IT'

Cassington, 1877

Although only twenty years old, Mary Hannah Allen was no stranger to death. The oldest of five children, Mary lost her mother when she was just nine years old and, when her father died shortly afterwards, Mary and her four brothers moved to Cassington to live with their grandparents, Mr and Mrs Putt. Unfortunately, Mrs Putt died when Mary was just sixteen and Mary took over the running of the house, caring for her grandfather and brothers.

By 1877, Mary had developed into an attractive and well-educated young woman, who was beginning to attract the attentions of a number of local suitors. Foremost among them was twenty-six-year-old Harry Rowles, the son of a prosperous farmer from nearby Kidlington. After a courtship of more than two years, punctuated by a large number of affectionate letters between the couple, there was an understanding that Mary and Harry would shortly be married.

Rowles was known locally to be somewhat unstable and his mother was firmly convinced that her son's abnormal behaviour was due to the fact that she had suffered a severe fright during her pregnancy. The boy was certainly extremely volatile and strong-willed throughout his childhood and possessed a fierce temper, which led to him being over-indulged by his friends and family, who were keen to escape the potentially explosive consequences of denying him his own way. Rowles's impulsive behaviour continued when he started an apprenticeship, at which time he tried to commit suicide by taking a draught of poison. Fortunately, he was quickly

The Green, Cassington. (Author's collection)

Kidlington, 1945. The home of Harry Rowles. (Author's collection)

given a powerful emetic, which induced him to vomit before the poison could have its intended effect.

Soon afterwards, Rowles ran away from home and enlisted in the Royal Artillery, but his military career was short-lived and he bought himself out. His unpredictable character had been the cause of much consternation during his brief period of service, as his fellow soldiers were constantly afraid that he might either harm them or himself. He now returned to his home village in possession of a service revolver, an acquisition that struck terror in the hearts of all who knew him.

When Rowles met Mary, he had just inherited the sum of £1,000, which he quickly frittered away, spending money freely on drink and on buying gifts to impress his new girlfriend. Although Mary's grandfather had initially welcomed the burgeoning romance, the young man's charms as a potential husband for his granddaughter quickly faded when Mr Putt realised that Rowles had no intention of seeking gainful employment and would therefore have no means of supporting Mary in marriage. Putt tried his hardest to make Rowles see the error of his ways and, when his efforts were unsuccessful, he turned his attentions to his granddaughter, begging her to give up Rowles and seek a more reliable husband.

Such a man was already showing an interest in courting Mary – the son of a farmer, baker and grocer from the village of Bladon – and, in July 1877, Mary broke off her relationship with Harry Rowles. Rowles, however, was not prepared to be so easily dismissed and continued to try and regain Mary's affections.

On 14 December 1877, Rowles spent most of the day drinking in a pub in Islip before going to Cassington to see Mary. Mary's grandfather was not at home at the time and, when he returned later that evening, it was to find Mary extremely upset. Tearfully, she told Mr Putt that Rowles had made threats against her and Putt took what she told him so seriously that, on the following morning, he approached a local magistrate and asked for protection for himself and his family.

Meanwhile, Rowles had spent the night drinking at a public house in Yarnton, from where he walked into Cassington and approached a villager, Mrs Hazel. Rowles asked her if she would go and see Mary and persuade her to see him, telling Mrs Hazel to be sure to say that he had not meant the hasty threats he had made towards Mary the previous evening. While Mrs Hazel set off on her errand, Rowles waited for her in the Red Lion public house, where he continued drinking.

Mrs Hazel returned to the pub with bad news. Mary was still very upset about the previous day's altercation between them and had no intention of ever speaking to him again. Not only that but she had told her grandfather everything and, at that very moment, he was in Oxford seeing a magistrate. Rowles appeared to accept the news quite calmly, asking Mrs Hazel how Mary was. Mrs Hazel was becoming concerned that Rowles might try to harm Mary but, when she questioned him, he insisted that nothing was further from his mind. 'I would not hurt a hair on her head nor anyone belonging to her,' he insisted, adding that he had too much regard for

The Red Lion, Cassington. (© N. Sly)

the family to even consider such an idea. He did, however, admit that he would like to have a few words with Mr Putt.

Regardless of Mary's wishes, Rowles finished his drink and set off to visit her. When he arrived at her cottage, Mary was alone apart from a servant, Lizzie Hall.

Mary reluctantly allowed her former fiancé into the house and Lizzie heard Rowles ask her if she had told her grandfather about the events of the previous evening. Although Lizzie didn't hear Mary's reply, she presumed that the answer was 'Yes', since Rowles immediately exclaimed, 'I shall be pulled! I shall be hung!'

'Oh, Harry dearest, what are you going to do?' asked Mary.

Hearing the obvious fear and distress in Mary's voice, Lizzie decided to go for help and ran out of the house. As she was explaining the situation to neighbours Mr and Mrs Green, they heard the sound of shots being fired from Putt's house, immediately followed by a woman's screams.

Edward Green bravely rushed into the house, finding the parlour door locked. He smashed a door panel and was confronted by a terrible sight. Mary Allen lay on her side on the floor, saturated with blood, while Rowles stood over her, still clutching a smoking gun, which he now pointed at Mr Green.

'If anyone comes to interfere with us, I'll shoot,' he threatened, at which Green immediately turned and left the house.

Outside, he bumped into Richard Lyford, who had heard the sound of gun shots and run to investigate. Lyford also went into the house and, when he asked Rowles to open the locked parlour door, he complied.

'I have shot her three times,' he told Lyford. 'She won't live, she will die.'
Lyford tried to persuade Rowles to hand over his gun but Rowles refused, although he did agree to accompany Lyford to the police house at Eynsham, to surrender himself to Constable Harrison. By now, Mrs Green was tending to Mary Allen, trying desperately to comfort the girl and to stem the blood that was pouring from her.

'How could you do such a thing?' she asked Rowles, who replied, 'She is my wife. I have a right to do what I like.'

Rowles and Lyford walked together towards Eynsham, with Rowles acting in a most disturbed and agitated manner, swinging his arms wildly and talking unusually fast. On their way, they met Mr Putt returning home from Oxford and Lyford persuaded Rowles to say nothing about the tragedy he would find there.

'You must be mad to do such a thing,' Lyford told Rowles as they continued their journey after parting with Mr Putt.

'Mad, Lyford? Why, I've been mad for some time,' replied Rowles. He continued to explain, 'I couldn't help it. The very Devil tempted me to do it. She has been very cruel and false to me and I have spent over £300 on her and also given her a gold watch and chain.' He concluded his explanation by asking Lyford to pray for him and Mary.

On their arrival at the police house, Constable Harrison took some convincing that the situation was not some terrible joke. It was only when Rowles emptied his pockets of the gun and cartridges, insisting that he had used them to shoot Mary

Allen that the truth sank in. Harrison walked Rowles 5 miles to Woodstock police station, noting that Rowles was talking continuously 'in a very wild way'. The constable handed him over to Inspector Bowen at Woodstock, whereupon Rowles immediately fell to the ground, apparently in the throes of a fit.

A doctor was called to examine him and was later to say that he believed that Rowles was suffering from epilepsy and that '… the coming on of a fit of that kind indicated mischief in the brain.' Rowles soon recovered and became noticeably calmer, telling the Inspector that what had happened between him and Mary was 'a horrible affair'. He expressed anxiety about some letters, which he believed would offer an explanation into his actions, asking the Inspector to ensure that they were retrieved from Mr Putt's house.

By then, a doctor had been summoned to attend to Mary Allen. He found her very weak due to loss of blood from three gunshot wounds, two to her arm and a third in her back, which had fractured her spine. Although she was too weak to give a deposition, she lingered for four days before finally losing her battle for life. An inquest into her death was convened before coroner Mr W.W. Robinson on 21 December, at which the jury recorded a verdict of 'wilful murder' against Harry Rowles.

Rowles was committed for trial at the Spring Assizes at Oxford before Mr Justice Baggallay. When his trial opened on 13 March, it soon became evident that not even his defence team of Mr Staveley Hill QC and Mr R.T. Reid were claiming that Rowles was innocent. Given that he was caught standing over Mary Allen with a smoking gun in his hand that would have been beyond the belief of any jury. Rather, the contentious issue at the trial was Rowles's mental state at the time of the shooting and whether or not he could be judged to have been criminally insane.

It was the contention of Mr Gough and Mr Sim, the prosecution counsels, that Rowles had shot Mary Allen out of jealousy, after she broke off their engagement and turned her attentions to another man. However, the defence produced witness after witness in an effort to prove that Rowles had not been in his right mind at the time of the murder and was thus not responsible for his actions, being unable to distinguish between right and wrong.

Both Richard Lyford and PC Harrison believed that Rowles had been completely mad in the immediate aftermath of the shooting and several of his friends and family members testified to his strange behaviour since childhood, which had become even more peculiar after he left the army.

Dr Tuke, a physician and expert on matters of lunacy, told the court that he had examined Rowles on two occasions and, both times, Rowles had exhibited a heavy, dull demeanour with insomnia and pronounced bouts of twitching. In Tuke's opinion, Rowles was suffering from a disorder of the brain and Tuke believed that his epileptic fit in the police station was a result of this disorder, rather than a consequence of agitation at having just killed someone. Rowles had spoken of seeing 'little black figures', which was judged to be a further symptom of his disease.

Mr Justice Baggallay asked Tuke if the prisoner's symptoms could be indicative of an excessive consumption of alcohol, but Tuke discounted that theory, stating that Rowles had appeared remarkably tranquil and had not exhibited any of the characteristic trembling and shaking associated with *delirium tremens* and alcohol withdrawal.

Next to take the witness stand was John Briscoe, a Fellow of the Royal College of Surgeons, who acted as surgeon at Oxford Gaol. Briscoe had seen Rowles constantly since his incarceration after the murder and had noticed only that he was suffering from insomnia. According to Briscoe, the prisoner always appeared completely natural and no different to any other person, his pulse was good and he was able to answer any questions rationally and calmly. Briscoe had made no special study of Rowles's mind because he hadn't deemed it necessary to do so. The only extra consideration he had given Rowles was to keep a close eye on him after a sharp nail was found in his clothing, with which, Briscoe believed, he had planned to commit suicide.

Prison governor Mr Cruikshank and Chaplain Reverend Thorp agreed with Briscoe's observations, both stating that they had always found Rowles sensible, rational and sane.

A number of letters written by Mary and Harry throughout the course of their relationship were introduced as evidence, with the prosecution contending that they illustrated Rowles's jealousy and the defence arguing that they were evidence of his insanity at the time.

One letter, written by Mary in March 1877, obviously referred to an argument between the couple after she had spoken to another man:

> ... As God is my witness, I will never speak to him or anyone else that you have objections to. I once more ask your forgiveness and remain, Your loving Polly. A thousand kisses. Do let me come and see you once more or I am sure I shall die.

Harry had replied a couple of days later, ending his letter, 'My lovely pet, if you do that and keep your word I can and will forgive you everything. I remain your affectionate Harry. Myriads of kisses.'

Mary had replied immediately, again promising to have nothing more to do with the other man:

> I hope you will make me as kind and loving husband as I think and hope and trust you will and I will try to be as good and loving a wife as ever a man had. Best love and kisses from your loving Polly.

However, by December of 1877, the tone of the letters between the couple had changed dramatically. Rowles wrote, 'Darling pet Polly, my heart is made easy and turned from all those horrible, cruel, wicked thoughts through your kind, loving affection towards me ...'

The letter continued to list a number of people whom Rowles believed had turned against him, ominously predicting:

Polly, dear, we shall see something bad sooner or later befall them. My darling, when I left you I was only one step at one time out of hell through those cruel, treacherous beings but God has turned my wrath and cleansed my mind and body from that impurity. But I will plump it out what the above sins were to have been.

A series of initials then denoted the people who Rowles had intended to 'shoot or kill in some way'.

After the introduction of the letters into court, yet more witnesses were called by the defence to demonstrate that Rowles had been delusional at the time of the shooting. Mrs Green related Rowles's insistence that he and Mary had been married and an employee from the *Oxford Journal* produced a notice from that newspaper that Rowles had submitted in 1875, announcing his marriage to a woman from Wisconsin. A pub landlord testified that, shortly before the murder, Rowles had told him that he had recently married and that his wife was currently in lodgings in Oxford. All of these accounts were patently untrue.

In his summary of the case for the jury, Mr Justice Baggallay gave them a detailed overview of the state of the defendant's mind almost from his early childhood to the day of the shooting, drawing the jury's attention to the often conflicting evidence of the various witnesses who had either known Rowles for a long time or had come into contact with him only after the murder. The judge dismissed the marriage announcement that had been placed in the newspaper, saying that it could have resulted from a delusion but could just as easily have been inserted for a joke or for some other unknown reason.

The church at Cassington, where Mary Allen is buried. (Author's collection)

Mary Allen's grave, Cassington churchyard. (© N. Sly)

The judge referred to the long, rambling letters written by Rowles both before and after his arrest, commenting that it was for the jury to determine whether they were written for a purpose or were the product of a wandering mind. Having carefully explained the legal definition of insanity, Mr Justice Baggallay suggested that it would have been beneficial to the case had some independent authority been called on to testify on the subject of madness. He reminded the jury of Rowles's epileptic fit at the police station and the fact that, after his recovery, he had expressed concern that his letters were recovered from Mary's home, saying that they would, '... clear up a good deal of what has passed'. How far was this conduct consistent with the definition of legal insanity – whether the prisoner knew right from wrong? After speaking for almost two and a half hours, Baggallay placed the case in the hands of the jury, advising them to take into account all the evidence they had heard in court to reach their verdict.

The jury retired, taking with them the correspondence between the defendant and Mary Allen, returning after seventy-five minutes with a verdict of 'guilty of wilful murder' against Harry Knowles. However, their verdict was tempered with a recommendation for mercy on the grounds of what they saw as extreme provocation, endured by Rowles at the hands of his errant fiancée.

Promising to forward the jury's recommendation to the appropriate authorities, the judge passed the death sentence on Rowles, advising him not to rely upon a favourable consideration but to prepare himself for death. Rowles accepted the sentence without reaction, the calm demeanour he had shown throughout the trial disturbed only by continued facial tics and nervous twitches.

The jury's recommendation for mercy came to nothing and Rowles was executed by William Marwood on 1 April 1878.

Note: There are some variations in accounts of the murder in the contemporary newspapers. Mary Hannah Allen is also named as either Mary Ann(e), Mary Hanna or Hanna Allen, while Rowles is referred to as both Harry and Henry. It seems most likely that his proper name was Henry but that he was usually known by the name Harry. I have taken the most commonly used names for this account and taken Mary Allen's correct name from her gravestone in Cassington churchyard.

13

'I WILL MAKE YOU SUFFER FOR IT BEFORE NIGHT'

Abingdon, 1885

The small cottage located in the narrow passage that ran along the north side of Ock Street in Abingdon was the scene of numerous violent arguments between its occupants, husband and wife John and Sarah Willoughby. The area around the cottage had resonated with the sound of the couple's incessant fights and quarrels for many years and indeed, in 1865, John Willoughby had viciously attacked his wife in the course of a marital disagreement and left her for dead. As a result of that assault, Willoughby had been sentenced to five years of penal servitude but, as soon as he was released from prison, he moved back in with Sarah, and their cat and dog existence resumed, almost as if they had never been apart.

Willoughby, who worked as a scavenger for the Urban Sanitary Authority, was described as having 'a morose disposition' and was known to be almost insanely jealous of his wife, without any apparent reason, accusing her of having a great many 'fancy men' about. He was frequently heard to threaten the long-suffering Sarah with violence or to promise to kill her in one way or another.

On 11 August 1885, the couple's next-door neighbour, Ann Allum, was talking to Sarah on her doorstep at eight o'clock in the morning when John Willoughby suddenly appeared and asked his wife if she would care to go for a walk with him. Sarah refused. John had been for a walk on the recent Bank Holiday and she had asked to accompany him then and been rebuffed.

Abingdon in 1905. (Author's collection)

'Very well,' said her husband, sulkily. 'I will make you suffer for it before night.' John Willoughby left the two women and as soon as he was safely out of earshot, Sarah turned to her neighbour and asked her what she thought she should do. 'If I was you, Mrs Willoughby, I would go,' Ann advised her but Sarah could be just as stubborn as her husband.

'I don't think I shall go today,' she finally decided.

The two neighbours saw each other again briefly at eleven o'clock that morning.

'Don't be frightened,' Sarah cheerfully told Ann, who replied, 'No, and don't you be frightened.' They were to be the last words she would ever address to her neighbour.

At about midday, John and his youngest son, ten-year-old William, were about to sit down to their lunch. An argument had been rumbling about the meal for some time and, as Sarah walked towards the kitchen table carrying a pie she had just baked, her husband stepped forward and, without saying a word, hit her hard on the top of her head with a coal hammer.

William heard his mother cry out, 'Oh dear, don't 'ee,' before he took to his heels and fled to fetch his older sister. Thirteen-year-old Mary ran back to the house with her brother to find her mother lying apparently dead on the brick floor of the kitchen, in a spreading pool of blood. Her father stood glowering behind the kitchen door and he and Mary looked at each other for a few moments without speaking until Mary rushed off in search of her older brother, fifteen-year-old Albert, who worked as a butcher's boy at a nearby shop.

Albert dashed to his parents' house, finding the door locked against him. With the assistance of a neighbour, greengrocer Isaac Porter, Albert forced the door open and found his mother lying on the kitchen floor with his father lying on his side nearby, a hammer and an open cut-throat razor close at hand. Isaac Porter knelt and picked up Sarah's hand. Finding that she was dead, he turned his attention to her husband, who had evidently cut his own throat. Porter spoke to John Willoughby but although Willoughby opened his eyes at the sound of Porter's voice, he quickly closed them again and made no reply.

The police were alerted and Superintendent Oliver Robotham was the first officer to arrive at the Willoughbys' home. Having checked that Sarah was beyond all assistance, the police officer turned her husband over so that he was lying on his back. Robotham found a cloth and bound up the deep wound that crossed Willoughby's throat from one side to the other, placing a pillow under his head to try and make him more comfortable.

Abingdon surgeon Mr Sidney Hayman arrived soon afterwards and, on removing the cloth from around Willoughby's throat, found that he had severed his windpipe and also had a small, star-shaped wound on the top of his head, probably the result of a fall.

Although the cut in Willoughby's throat was a deep one, he had somehow managed to avoid cutting any major blood vessels and Hayman arranged for him to be conveyed under police guard to the Radcliffe Infirmary in Oxford. He was expected to make a full recovery although, seemingly determined to commit suicide, he persisted in tearing the bandages from his throat and, had it not been for the efforts of the constables guarding him, would have reopened his wound and, in all probability, would subsequently have bled to death.

Hayman conducted a post-mortem examination on the body of fifty-two-year-old Sarah Willoughby and found that she had been struck on the head with the hammer, fracturing her skull and pulverising her brain beneath. Her attacker had used such force in hitting her that the hammer head had penetrated her brain to a depth of 1in, which would have killed her instantly. There were no signs of any struggle or resistance on Sarah's part and the surgeon theorised that she had been attacked while standing up and that the single blow inflicted on her head would have pole-axed her where she stood.

An inquest into Sarah Willoughby's death was opened at the Guildhall in Abingdon by Borough coroner Mr Bromley Challenor. The jury heard from the Willoughbys' three children, who gave their accounts of the events of 11 August. The youngest boy, William, added that he had never seen his father strike his mother before, nor had he ever heard him threaten her with violence. Mary, however, had heard her father making threats, telling her mother that, if it wasn't for the children, he would do something to her.

Mary was accustomed to her parents' constant fighting but added that they had been quarrelling a little more than usual over the past week or so. Albert did not believe his father had ill-treated his mother, although he was aware of his father's previous conviction for an assault on Sarah and admitted that the couple had not lived happily together for some time. Albert also testified about his father's recent strange behaviour, which included making allegations that 'someone' was putting poison in his tea.

The Willoughbys' neighbours also testified to the unhappiness of the couple's relationship. Ann Allum related her conversation with Sarah on the morning of the murder, saying that she had often heard the Willoughbys fighting and arguing.

Isaac Porter stated that he had frequently heard John threaten Sarah in the past and, earlier on the day of the murder, had heard John shouting in the street at Sarah, 'Madam, I'll do for you before long'. He had taken no notice, being used to witnessing the couple's very public grievances aired in the full view and hearing of the entire neighbourhood.

Several of the neighbours made a point of stating that John Willoughby was known to act very strangely at times and some even went as far as to suggest that he should have been placed under restraint many years ago, since he was no longer mentally capable of taking full responsibility for his actions.

The inquest then heard from Inspector Robotham and surgeon Sidney Hayman, before the jury returned a verdict of wilful murder against John Willoughby, who was committed for trial on a coroner's warrant for the murder of his wife.

His trial opened at Oxford on 29 October 1885 before Mr Justice Field. Mr A.J. Ram and Mr J.G. Smith prosecuted the case and, at the judge's request, Mr Gough defended John Willoughby, who pleaded 'Not Guilty' to the charge of murder against him.

The evidence presented at court deviated very little from that heard at the inquest, with only one major difference. Whereas the coroner's court was not empowered to take into consideration Willoughby's mental state at the time of the murder, the court of law was. The fact that John had been arguing with Sarah on the morning of her death and had ended the argument by striking her on the head with a hammer was not disputed, which meant that the only real question for the jury to debate was whether or not Willoughby's actions arose from insanity.

Willoughby had been examined twice in prison by Dr C. Bastien, who found him to be suffering from a number of delusions. Willoughby believed that people in the street could read his mind and that poisons were entering his house through keyholes and cracks in the walls. He complained of constant pains in his head and insomnia and Bastien believed that he was suffering from a defect of reason which would prevent him from knowing what he was doing at the time of the murder and of appreciating the consequences of his actions.

The jury needed less than five minutes to decide that John Willoughby's state of mind rendered him not responsible for his actions in the eyes of the law and they returned a verdict of 'Guilty but insane', leaving the judge to order that he should be detained as a lunatic in Oxford Prison, until his Majesty's pleasure be known.

In 1891, a widower named John Willoughby appears on the list of names of residents at the Broadmoor Lunatic Asylum and, ten years later, a John Willoughby with an identical personal history appears on the list of inmates of a workhouse in Pontefract in Yorkshire, dying in 1905. Whether or not these records relate to the John Willoughby featured in this chapter cannot be positively confirmed.

Note: In some contemporary accounts of the murder, Albert Willoughby is alternatively named Alfred.

14

'I BELIEVE OLD BECKLEY LIES DEAD UP THE ROAD THERE UNDER A TREE'

Blenheim Palace, Woodstock, 1885

William Beckley was employed as a blacksmith on the Blenheim estate, near Woodstock. Beckley, who lived with his daughter, Sarah Ann, at Water Meadow Gate was nearing retirement age and had recently been receiving treatment for a heart condition from the local doctor.

In the summer of 1885, William Beckley had a falling out with another of the estate workers, sixty-three-year-old George Boddington. The two men argued heatedly about a tar brush that had gone missing and, once the brush had been found, Boddington picked it up and swiped it down the front of Beckley's shirt. Their immediate boss, George Thompson, was exasperated at such juvenile behaviour from two men in their sixties and told them to stop larking about and get on with their work otherwise he would sack them both.

The spat between the two men seemed to have passed and they continued to work together without any outward signs of lingering animosity between them. However, on 12 August, some four or five weeks after the original disagreement, the two men were sent to tar some railings. George Thompson saw them both at work that morning, as did other estate employees, and there seemed to be no indications of any squabbling.

Woodstock. (Author's collection)

At two o'clock in the afternoon, George Boddington arrived at the home of Mr Wilkins, a lodge keeper on the estate.

'I believe old Beckley lies dead up the road there under a tree,' Boddington said casually. Mr Wilkins and his wife went straight to the place indicated by Boddington and found William Beckley lying face down on the grass in a pool of blood.

Wilkins sent for the police and a doctor, while Mrs Wilkins sent her sister, Mrs White, to alert Sarah Ann Beckley of the tragedy. When Sarah Ann arrived at the scene, she went through the pockets of her father's clothes and pulled out his purse, which still contained his money. Whoever had killed William Beckley had obviously not had robbery as a motive.

When the police arrived, they brought with them George Saunders, who took some of the earliest recorded scene-of-crime photographs. Dr McClure pronounced William Beckley dead then performed a post-mortem examination, from which he concluded that the dead man had received two heavy blows on his head from a blunt instrument. Beckley's nose was broken and a large, deep gash extended across his cheek to his jaw. A further blow had shattered his skull, reducing his brain beneath almost to a pulp. At an inquest into Beckley's death, held at the George and Dragon public house at Long Handborough, the coroner's jury returned a verdict of wilful murder by some person or persons unknown.

However, even before the end of the inquest, the police had a suspect in custody – George Boddington – who Inspector Oakley refused outright to produce at the inquest before the coroner. Interviewed at his work on the day after the murder,

A worker's cottage, Blenheim Park, 1918. (Author's collection)

Boddington had stated to Inspector Oakley that he had found the deceased man when he returned to his tarring job after his dinner break. Oakley asked Boddington if he and Beckley had been on friendly terms.

'Sometimes,' replied Boddington guardedly and went on to agree with the Inspector that Beckley had died from violence rather than a natural death. He told Oakley that, on the previous day, the two men had been tarring together and that he had gone to the gas house to fetch some more tar. When he returned with it, Beckley had complained that the tar contained water and couldn't be used.

'Did he resist forcibly?' asked the Inspector, to which Boddington replied, 'No.' Inspector Oakley noted that Boddington seemed very nervous and was trembling violently as he answered the questions. Close to where he was working was a spade, the blade of which had been dipped in tar, as if to conceal bloodstains, as well as an iron bracket.

Boddington was taken to the police station at Woodstock for further questioning and later charged with the murder. His clothes were taken from him for closer examination, although Boddington was quick to point out that, if any blood was found on them, it would have come from when he helped to place Beckley's body on the cart.

George Boddington was remanded in custody at Oxford Prison, where he placed an urgent request to see the prison chaplain. The Reverend F.J. Chavasse obliged and found that the prisoner now wanted to make a formal statement about Beckley's death.

According to Boddington, the two men had argued about the water in the tar and Beckley had infuriated Boddington by calling him a scamp and a vagabond. Boddington, who had an axe in his hand at the time, lashed out at Beckley in temper and, realising that he had killed him, went to seek help from Mr Wilkins, throwing the axe away as he walked. It was later found by the police under a tree, close to the scene of the murder.

After appearing before magistrates at the Town Hall in Woodstock, George Boddington was committed for trial at the next Oxford Assizes. The proceedings opened on 27 October 1885 before Mr Justice Field, with Mr Darling and Mr Mowbray appearing for the prosecution and Mr Stuart Sim appearing for Boddington.

It emerged that Sarah Ann Beckley, the victim's daughter, had once been engaged to Boddington but they had fallen out about money on the eve of their marriage and the wedding had been called off.

After that revelation, much of the trial was taken up with demonstrating that George Boddington had a long history of mental illness and was thus not of sound mind when the murder was committed.

One of the chief witnesses was Mr Heurtley Sankey, the medical superintendent of Littlemore Asylum. Sankey produced records dating back to 1852, which showed that George Boddington had been an inmate. Boddington had once been a police constable in London but had been discharged from the force for drunkenness, having previously been warned several times about similar incidences.

He had first been admitted to the asylum on 18 July 1852, after arriving in Oxford, apparently from the capital. Having been observed wandering the streets of Oxford for some time, the police were called, at which Boddington had become very violent and it had taken five officers to restrain him. Quiet and apparently subdued for a time, he had suddenly erupted again and broke several windows at the police station before he could be brought under control. He was strapped down and cold water was poured over him, before he was taken to the asylum in a straitjacket.

He was admitted to the asylum again on 16 August that year, at which time records showed that he had suffered 'a loss of mind'. Discharged on 27 November, he apparently lived the rest of his life in fear of being readmitted.

His daughter, Mrs Clara Rowles, testified that her father had once been an under-gamekeeper on the estate but had been accidentally shot in the face and had lost an eye. This had made him extremely nervous and the wound had not healed properly – shot was still being removed from the injury even recently. Boddington had been widowed in 1873 and had never got over the death of his wife.

In recent times, he had begun to act very strangely and had been convinced that people were going to take him away somewhere or take him back to Littlemore. On several occasions he had shaved and then sat down and waited for the mysterious 'people' to come for him. He frequently said goodbye to his family in the morning, adding that they probably wouldn't see him again as someone was going to take him away. Sometimes, he insisted on taking his six-year-old grandson with him, believing that he wouldn't be taken anywhere if the boy was there.

It was noted that Boddington's mother had also been a patient at Littlemore in 1862, when she had been admitted suffering from 'mental excitement'. Judged as being a danger to others on her admission, she had been discharged three months later as 'improved'. This, according to the defence, was evidence of inherited insanity.

Thus, the entire case hinged on the question of Boddington's mental state. The prosecution argued that Boddington's actions after the murder had been those of a rational, sane man, while the defence insisted that their client had clearly been insane at the time of the killing. The defence's argument was even supported by a prosecution witness, Dr C. Bastien, a physician from London, who had examined Boddington at the request of the prosecution and believed him to have been insane on the day of the murder.

In his summary of the evidence for the jury, Mr Justice Field clearly explained the legal definitions of insanity saying that, in order to be deemed insane, it must be clearly proved that, at the time of committing the act, the accused must have been labouring under such a defect of reasoning from a disease of the mind that he didn't know the nature or quality of the act he was committing or know that what he was doing was wrong.

The jury retired for half an hour, returning to pronounce George Boddington 'Guilty' of the wilful murder of William Beckley. However, they made a strong recommendation for mercy on the grounds of Boddington's age and his infirmities, which the judge promised to forward to the appropriate authorities. Boddington's daughter fainted as the judge then proceeded to pronounce sentence of death on her father.

Days later, it was announced that George Boddington had been reprieved and he died in prison two years later.

15

'I HAVE GOT A DEAD 'UN THIS MORNING'

Brasenose Common, Headington, 1887

The lifestyle of gypsy families in 1887 was not one to be envied. The travelling people were at the mercy of the weather all year round, whether the heat of summer or the bitter cold of winter. Forced to scratch a living in any way they could, many supplemented their meagre income with a little poaching or petty theft. Thus they were very rarely welcomed in any area and were always in fear of the local police who almost invariably moved them on wherever they tried to settle.

The Smith family were perhaps a little more legitimate than some of their contemporaries, since Mrs Lucy Smith had a valid pedlar's certificate from the Thame Police and, in order to have been awarded this certificate, she would have to have proved herself to be 'of good character'. The licence entitled her to offer goods for sale to the public and she used it to good effect to sell the pegs, baskets and other items fashioned by her husband, Charlie.

Charlie and Lucy travelled around Oxfordshire with their two children, seventeen-year-old Oceana – usually known as Oshey – and her eleven-year-old brother, Prince Albert. Charlie was known as a particularly violent man, who regularly beat both Lucy and the children, using either his fists or a stout stick. At one point, Lucy had been sufficiently worried by his abusive behaviour to make a formal complaint to magistrates at Witney. However, she had never followed up her complaint and continued to live with her husband, in spite of his ill treatment of her.

In February 1887, the Smiths had set up camp on common land near Headington, pitching a makeshift tent fashioned from old blankets close to a stream so that they would have a convenient water supply. They had camped there before and had become acquainted with George and Kate Smith (no relation), who lived in a nearby cottage. George and Kate would visit them and on the afternoon of 18 February, it was obvious to George that Lucy had recently been severely beaten. When he asked Charlie what had happened, Charlie explained that he was jealous of something that Lucy had done almost thirty years previously.

'Let it go. Forgive her,' George advised Charlie, who stubbornly insisted that he would not and continued tending his fire. The kettle boiled and tea was made, at which Lucy asked Charlie for a bit of 'baccy'. Charlie merely growled at his wife, who quickly moved as far away from him as she could. Kate Smith took pity on her and managed to persuade Charlie to give her a bit of tobacco, which she then passed to Lucy. Kate tried to coax her into the tent, out of the biting cold, but Lucy seemed too afraid to go anywhere near her husband.

She was eventually persuaded into the tent when it came time for the family to retire for the night but at about four o'clock on the morning of 19 February, Oshey woke with a start to hear her father, who was once again shouting at her mother.

As Oshey watched, he snatched up the hammer he used for his peg making and began to beat Lucy about her head, back and legs. The vigorous beating continued until Charlie was too tired to carry on, at which point he fell back exhausted onto his straw bed and went straight to sleep.

Lucy crawled out of the tent to go to the stream for water. Oshey waited a while for her to return and, when she didn't, went to check, finding her mother lying dead on the banks of the stream.

As Oceana tried in vain to rouse her mother, Charlie himself came out of the tent and, realising that he had killed his wife, fell to his knees by her body, sobbing piteously and repeating the words, 'My wench, my wench.'

Headington, 1916, near where Charlie Smith attacked his wife. (Author's collection)

Old Headington.

Oshey seized the opportunity to grab Prince Albert and make a run for it. She arrived at the Smiths' cottage at just before eight o'clock in the morning, pounding on the door with her fists and calling, 'Missus! Missus!' When the Smiths answered the door, she dragged her brother into their cottage, telling the startled couple, 'My mother's dead. He's killed her with a hammer.'

George Smith paused only to put some clothes on before rushing to see what had happened. As he approached the camp, he could see Lucy lying on the ground like a bundle of rags. 'My old woman's dead,' Charlie told him. 'She fell down outside the tent. What's to be done now?'

George told Charlie that he would go for a doctor but instead returned with two policemen. Charlie greeted them calmly, saying, 'Good morning. I have got a dead 'un this morning. My wife is dead.'

Having examined the body of Lucy Smith and seen the extent of her head injuries and the amount of blood she appeared to have lost, Sergeant Quarterman took a firm hold of Charlie Smith and informed him that he was under arrest for the wilful murder of his wife, asking him where he had hidden the murder weapon.

'I have no hammer,' protested Smith tellingly, insisting that his wife had simply fallen over. PC Sly began a search for a murder weapon and soon found a bloodied hammer concealed under the straw in the tent, on which the Smith family slept. 'That's my hammer,' Charlie now admitted. 'My peg hammer.'

Lucy's body was taken to the Original Swan Inn nearby, where a post-mortem examination revealed that she had died from head injuries, which could not possibly have been caused by a fall. Meanwhile, Smith was taken before magistrates, where he continued to deny having played any part in his wife's death.

The chief witness against him was his daughter, Oshey, who gave her account of the events of 17/18 February, including the fact that she had seen her father strike her mother. Charlie was permitted to question the witnesses and asked just one question of Oshey – did she see him striking his wife?

'Yes, in the tent,' Oshey quickly replied.

'No, no. No such thing, my dear child,' argued Charlie but the magistrates chose to believe Oshey's version rather than her father's and Charles Smith was committed for trial at the next assizes at Reading. The trial took place before Baron Huddlestone in April 1887 and in spite of the defence's argument that the death of Lucy Smith was manslaughter, it was wilful murder that the jury decided that Smith was guilty of.

On 9 May 1887, sixty-three-year-old Charles Smith faced hangman James Berry at Oxford Prison with characteristic bravado, telling Berry that there was no need for him to put the straps on when it came time for him to be pinioned. However, his cockiness deserted him as he walked to the scaffold – he fainted and had to be carried to the drop and supported until it fell beneath him. He went to his death without ever revealing the motive for his wife's murder.

16

'I HOPE I'VE MADE A GOOD JOB OF IT'

In 1887, Joseph Walker worked as a saddler in the town of Chipping Norton, although he was more often to be found in one of the local public houses than at his work. In common with his second wife, Henrietta, to whom he had been married for ten years, Joseph enjoyed a drink and their frequent binges often led to fierce quarrels between them.

More than once, the local police had to separate them and Joseph had appeared before magistrates several times for assaulting Henrietta after a drunken argument, on one occasion serving two months in prison. When Joseph's eldest son hung himself at his place of employment in Croydon, Joseph drank more and more in an effort to 'drown his sorrows'.

On 16 September 1887, Joseph was walking around Chipping Norton searching for Henrietta. He complained to Thomas Gardner that he had been out working all day but he knew that when he got home, Henrietta would accuse him of drinking and sleeping with prostitutes. She was such a liar, said Joseph, that if he caught hold of her that night, he would put an end to her to stop her lies for ever.

Gardner wasn't quite sure whether to take Walker seriously or not. Nevertheless, he advised him to think carefully about what he was saying and to cool off for a couple of hours before returning home. Joseph appeared to heed his advice, shaking Gardner's hand gratefully, with tears streaming from his eyes.

Minutes later, Gardner happened to bump into Henrietta who was chatting in the street to the local chimney sweep. Gardner thought it only fair to warn her

Chipping Norton. (Author's collection)

that her husband was in a terrible mood and had threatened to 'do for her' when he got home. As he had done to Joseph, Gardner urged Henrietta not to go home straight away – advice that she chose to ignore.

When she got home, Joseph was waiting for her and it quickly became apparent to their children that both of their parents had been drinking. A noisy argument began as soon as Henrietta walked through the door and their eldest daughter, Julia, who was in service to a local family, decided to leave them to it and spend the night at her place of work.

Now the subject of the argument turned to the suicide of Joseph's eldest son, with each blaming the other for the boy's death. The argument was witnessed by the couple's youngest son, also named Joseph, and his two young cousins, until Joseph senior suddenly seemed to realise that they were present and asked his son to take the younger children to bed. Young Joseph was only too glad to escape the battle zone but he had not been upstairs for long when he heard two bloodcurdling screams.

He ran back downstairs again to see his stepmother lying on the floor, with his father kneeling on her. As Joseph watched in horror, his father pulled a bloody knife from his wife's neck and shouted, 'I've done it!'

With that, he jumped to his feet and rushed out of the house to his neighbour, Robert Sharman, to tell him what had just happened. Sharman and his son immediately went to see if they could help Henrietta but found her lying face down on the floor, obviously dead. Meanwhile, Joseph junior had run off in search of a policeman, eventually finding Superintendent Cope on a patrol of the town.

When Joseph told Cope what he had just seen, Cope instructed him to return home and await the arrival of the police at the house. While Joseph did as he was told, Cope rushed back to the police station for back-up, arriving at the Walkers' home with two police constables. There they found Joseph Walker and his father waiting for them.

As Cope examined Henrietta's body for signs of life, her husband asked, 'Is she dead?' adding, 'I think I've made a good job of it. I hope I've made a good job of it.' Dr Hutchinson arrived minutes later to confirm that he had indeed 'made a good job of it', cutting Henrietta's throat so deeply that she was almost decapitated.

The knife that Walker had used was retrieved from the ash pan and Walker was arrested and charged with the wilful murder of his wife. He was brought to trial at the Oxford Assizes in October 1887, before Mr Justice Hawkins. Mr J.D.S. Sim and Mr Lawrence Jackson prosecuted the case, while Walker was defended by Mr R. Acland.

The crux of the case was the degree of provocation that Walker had endured before plunging the knife into his wife's throat, with the defence insisting that Henrietta had attacked Joseph first and his passion had been so aroused that he had retaliated by stabbing her. Thus it was the contention of the defence team that Walker's offence was manslaughter rather than that of wilful murder, with which he was charged.

Chipping Norton police station. (© N. Sly)

On his arrest, the police had noted that Walker had what was described in court as 'a slight scratch' on his face. There had, of course, been no eyewitnesses to the events immediately preceding the murder but Joseph junior had been an ear witness and, although he had not heard anything to indicate an attack on his father by his stepmother on this occasion, he testified in court that he had often seen Henrietta threaten his father with a knife in the past and had once heard her say that she would stab him.

However, as Mr Justice Hawkins pointed out while summarising the evidence for the jury, Walker had not raised this line of defence before, neither in his statements to the police nor at his appearance before the magistrates. The 'slight scratch' was hardly evidence of a knife attack on Joseph by Henrietta and a verbal argument between the couple would not constitute sufficient provocation to justify a reduction in the charge from murder to manslaughter. Walker had also made threats against his wife to other people earlier that evening, saying that he would 'do for her' and 'put an end to her'.

The jury needed little time for deliberation before returning a verdict of 'Guilty', albeit with a recommendation of mercy for Walker. Promising to bring the jury's recommendation to the attention of the relevant authorities, Mr Justice Hawkins remarked that he viewed the crime that Walker had committed as 'cruel, wicked and merciless', before donning the black cap and passing a sentence of death.

Within a week, Walker's case was taken up by the Howard Association, an organisation founded in 1866 and named after John Howard, the founder of the penal reform movement. The aims of the organisation were the advancement of the most efficient means of penal treatment and crime prevention, in addition to reformatory and preventive treatment of offenders, with the ultimate goal of the abolition of the death penalty.

In a letter to the then Home Secretary, Henry Matthews, the chairman and the secretary of the Howard Association called Matthews's attention to what they called the 'extreme and long-repeated provocation' of Joseph Walker by his wife in the run-up to her murder. The writers stated that 'a lady at Oxford' had informed them that Henrietta Walker was 'so drunken and so cruel and violent to himself and to his children by a former wife that his provocation was enough to madden any man.'

The letter continued to tell Matthews that, on the day of the murder, Henrietta had 'rifled his pockets, while asleep, of all his money and struck him so as to cause a wound and bruises and went out and got drunk.'

Finally, Francis Peek (Chairman) and William Tallack (Secretary) informed Matthews that Walker regarded Henrietta's conduct as having driven his 'favourite' son to commit suicide.

Regardless of the recommendation from the jury or the impassioned letter from the Howard League, the Home Secretary declined to interfere with the course of justice and Joseph Walker was executed by former policeman James Berry at Oxford Prison on 15 November 1887.

17

'THERE WILL BE A RUM JOB PRESENTLY'

Milton-under-Wychwood, 1888

The 23 May 1888 had apparently been a normal day for builder's labourer Robert Upton, who had been working at Shipton Court. The only thing remotely out of the ordinary was a remark made by sixty-one-year-old Upton to one of his fellow workmen as he left the site. 'There will be a rum job presently,' Upton told the man in passing, offering no explanation as to the meaning of his words or the nature of the 'rum job' he was anticipating.

Upton walked back to his home in Milton-under-Wychwood in the company of another workmate. Nothing more was said about any 'rum jobs' before the two men parted company outside Upton's cottage.

Yet within seconds of Robert Upton's arrival at home, his sixty-six-year-old wife, Emma, rushed from the house, screaming that her husband had threatened to kill her. A near neighbour, Mr Miles, who was drawn to the Uptons' house by Emma's yells, watched in horror as Robert Upton suddenly erupted from the cottage and chased his wife across the yard, waving a thick iron bar that was almost 3ft long over his head.

As Robert caught up with the fleeing Emma, he swung his fist at her and knocked her down. As she tumbled, Robert lost his balance and fell with her, banging her head hard against the ground.

Miles and other neighbours immediately rushed to aid the unfortunate Emma, managing to wrest the iron bar out of her husband's grasp and throw it to one side out of his reach. As soon as Robert was pulled away from Emma, he seemed

*Shipton Court,
Shipton-under-
Wychwood, where
Robert Upton
worked. (Author's
collection)*

*Milton-under-
Wychwood.
(© R. Sly)*

to quieten down. However, his calm demeanour was just an illusion as moments later Robert wriggled free from his captors and grabbed the bar again.

Emma had by this time risen groggily to her feet. Seeing Robert in possession of the bar again, she tried desperately to escape him but her efforts were useless. As her neighbours looked on, Robert swung the bar, catching Emma across the side of her face. Emma fell to the ground again and Robert managed to hit her two or three times more on the head before the horrified bystanders managed to disarm him.

The police were sent for and Robert was handed over into their custody. Emma had died almost instantly and a later post-mortem examination would show that her skull was almost pulverised and one of her arms badly broken. Informed of the death of his wife, Upton expressed satisfaction, saying that it was a good job. He told the police that he had meant to do it, and would happily go to the gallows like a prince.

Under questioning, Upton made no attempt to deny having killed his wife – on the contrary, he seemed highly delighted to have done so and pronounced himself quite prepared to face the consequences of his act. The only comment he made about his wife was that he hoped she had gone to heaven.

Upton was brought before magistrates at Chipping Norton, charged with the wilful murder of his wife and eventually committed for trial at the next Oxford Assizes, which opened at the end of June.

The trial was presided over by Mr Justice Denman, with Mr J.O. Stuart Sim and Mr R. Acland prosecuting. Although he had made numerous statements to the police, in which he admitted to the murder, when his trial opened, Upton pleaded 'Not Guilty' and, at the judge's request, Mr Mackarness was appointed to defend him.

Emma Upton was known to be a quiet, inoffensive woman but it emerged in court that she had left her husband on two separate occasions, once at Christmas in 1887 and once shortly before the murder. All of the witnesses to the frenzied attack on her agreed that Robert Upton was 'in a state of very great excitement' and it was the contention of the defence that Upton was not responsible for his actions at the time of the murder. Mr Mackarness spoke eloquently in Upton's defence, telling the jury that Emma's death was not premeditated and that at most, the charge against her husband should be one of manslaughter rather than wilful murder. However, the fact that Upton had commented on a 'rum job' well before the murder belied the defence counsel's words and the jury needed little time for deliberation before finding him guilty as charged.

Upton was sentenced to death and hanged at Oxford Castle by James Berry on 17 July 1888. Berry made a poor job of calculating the necessary length of rope for the task and Upton was almost decapitated, as the executioner tried to hang him with a drop of only 5ft. It is said that, when Upton's body was taken down after the hanging for the customary post-mortem examination, his neck had stretched by more than 12in.

Such was the outrage at the botched execution that questions were asked in parliament. The Home Secretary assured the house that such 'deplorable accidents' were very rare – in fact there had only been two reported since 1878. Mr Brookfield MP asked if Dr Marshall's new 'contrivance' had been considered for future executions, since it purported to produce instantaneous death with a drop of only 3ft. Home Secretary Henry Matthews replied that Dr Marshall's suggestion was known to the authorities but he didn't think that it would have the desired effects in eliminating such unfortunate occurrences. (In fact, the Home Office went on to issue an official table of execution 'drops' in 1892.) In answer to a further question from Mr Brookfield, Matthews stated that he did not believe that the Departmental Committee appointed to enquire into the matter had considered the merits of the electrical method of executing criminals.

Note: Some contemporary newspaper accounts give Upton's forename as Thomas.

18

'I COULD NOT HURT THE POOR CREATURE'

Henley-on-Thames, 1893

In 1893, Lambridge House near Henley-on-Thames was a weekend retreat owned by Mr Henry Joseph Mash. Mr Mash had a fruiterer's shop in Glasshouse Lane, Piccadilly Circus and, during the week, he and his family lived in Redcliffe Gardens, London. While the Mash family was not in residence, Lambridge was left in the sole charge of thirty-year-old governess and housekeeper, Miss Kate Laura Dungey. The small farm on the estate was run by George Dawson but, once he left work for the day, Kate was usually alone on the premises, apart from two boys who worked on the farm and slept in the house each night. Miss Dungey had worked for the Mash family for around seven years and was a trusted servant. Described as a woman of 'very superior attainments', she was good looking, with a fine figure, and was also an accomplished pianist, with a beautiful singing voice.

On 8 December 1893, the two boys, thirteen-year-old James Froome and his eleven-year-old brother, Harry, finished work for the day then went to their home in Assendon. At around half past eight at night, they returned to Lambridge House to sleep but could get no reply to their knocks on the door, even though they could see a light burning in the kitchen. The boys went to sit in the well house for an hour or so before renewing their efforts to get inside the house. They walked all around the building, shouting for Miss Dungey and eventually looked through a glass panel in the kitchen door. They could see no sign of the housekeeper, but could see the kitchen clock, the hands of which were at ten minutes to ten. Eventually, James and Harry decided to walk back to Assendon and tell their father that they were unable to get indoors to their beds.

When his sons arrived back on his doorstep, John Froome immediately went with James to see George Dawson, who lived at Box Folly, near Assendon. Dawson had already retired to bed by the time they arrived but he got up and, picking up a swordstick, accompanied them back to Lambridge. There he found all the doors locked, exactly as James had said they were.

It was unusual for Miss Dungey to lock the house doors. Although she was often alone in the house, she always insisted that she never felt afraid and, had she wanted to, she could have slept at Mr Mash's other home in Henley, where other servants were employed. Now, Dawson and the Froomes tried both the front door and the kitchen door then walked around the house to tap on Miss Dungey's bedroom window. There was no response. Dawson then went to check on the dog, a black retriever, which was chained in the yard. Normally, the dog would welcome him enthusiastically but now it was lying very still and appeared drowsy, as if it had been doped.

The men went back to the house and only then did Dawson notice that the bay window to the sitting room was open. James insisted that it had not been open earlier, saying that he and his brother had walked all around the house with lanterns and would have noticed. Dawson and the Froomes climbed through the window to gain entrance to the house.

Initially, everything seemed just as it always was, with nothing out of place. The men went through the house to the kitchen, where a lamp burned and Miss Dungey's knitting lay abandoned on the kitchen table next to the tea things. Worryingly, there was what looked like a bloodstain on the door handle and a broken and bloody stick lay on the floor.

James remembered that he and his brother had heard a strange noise earlier coming from the woods around the property, which he described as sounding like the growl of a cat with a mouse. Carrying their lanterns, the men followed his directions to the spot in the wood where he believed the noise had come from. There they found Kate Dungey lying on the very edge of the wood, about 30 yards from the house – in fact the Froomes would later say that Dawson walked straight to the body, almost as if he knew in advance where to find it!

Kate lay on her back, with one arm raised and her legs bent, a poker still tightly clutched in one of her hands. There was blood on her neck and pooled around her body and, according to Dawson, her head appeared somehow 'twisted'. Close to the body lay a 'rammer' – an instrument used to mash pig food, which was over 4ft long and so heavy that it needed two hands to lift it. Dawson was so terrified that he didn't stop to see if Kate was still breathing but harnessed the pony and trap and drove as fast as he could to Henley to fetch the police and a doctor.

Superintendent Keal met Dawson at Henley police station. By then, Dawson was in such a state of nervous agitation that he could barely speak but he finally managed to tell the Superintendent: 'The housekeeper at Lambridge has been murdered today.' Keal and a constable accompanied Dawson back to the house and, since it was now raining and hailing heavily, they carried Miss Dungey's body from

Henley-on-Thames. (Author's collection)

the woods into the kitchen. When the police conducted a search of the premises, they found a scattering of women's hair pins and a brooch in the hall, along with a broken lamp glass and several spots of blood. A candlestick and a box of matches lay on the floor, both of which were bloodstained.

The police surmised that Miss Dungey had been surprised in the hall and had struggled desperately with her attacker or attackers, seizing the poker to defend herself. She had then tried to flee from the house and had been pursued towards the woods, where she was ultimately killed. Inexplicably, after conducting an initial search of the property, Superintendent Keal and the constable then left, entrusting the keys of the house to George Dawson. The police returned to the house the next morning to resume their investigations. At that time, a footprint was seen in a flower bed outside the drawing room window and Keal instructed Dawson to cover it up to protect it.

Surgeon Mr George Smith examined Miss Dungey's body on the morning after its discovery, finding her to be covered with both dirt and blood. When she was washed, twenty-four wounds were revealed on her head, neck, arms and hands. She also had numerous bruises all over her body. Smith believed that the wounds had been made by two different weapons. Those on her head, arms and hands had been inflicted with a blunt instrument such as a stick or the rammer, while something sharp, such as a knife, had caused the wounds on her neck. Smith believed that Miss Dungey had died some hours before she was found – most probably at between five and eight o'clock – and that her death would not have been instantaneous but that she might have survived the attack on her for some time. Smith also stated that the blows rained on the victim could even have been inflicted by a woman and there were no signs of any attempted violation.

An inquest was opened on 11 December before the deputy coroner for South Oxfordshire, Mr Augustus Jones. The proceedings were held at Lambridge, where farmer Walter Dungey identified his daughter's body, telling the inquest that Kate had always spoken of being happy in her job and had not minded being in the house alone. As far as he was aware, his daughter did not have a boyfriend.

Henry Mash then told the coroner that, although he had made a thorough search of the house, he had been able to find nothing missing. Kate Dungey had recently been paid and, although her pockets had been turned out, the police found four or five sovereigns in her handbag at the house and thus discounted robbery as the motive for her murder.

The coroner's jury heard Kate described as '...the most amiable and inoffensive woman imaginable', although it was revealed at the inquest that, in the past, she had had arguments with several people. One of these was George Dawson. Mr Mash told the inquest that Dawson had wanted to live at Lambridge and had offered to pay rent to do so. Miss Dungey had not been at all happy about the prospect and Mash stated that he believed there had later been some sort of disagreement between her and Dawson about money matters.

Dawson dismissed the argument as trivial, saying that it had been nothing more than a few words over some washing, which had occurred three months earlier. It was certainly not a wrangle and scarcely even a difference – Dawson insisted that he had been on friendly terms with Miss Dungey right up until the last time he saw her alive, which was at around half past four on the afternoon of her death. Dawson did, however, recall an incident that had occurred during the previous summer. He had been out and, when he returned, he found Kate crying in the kitchen. She told him that there had been 'a rare scene' between Mr and Mrs Mash and that Mrs Mash had tried to strike her with an umbrella, only being prevented from doing so by Mr Mash, who stepped between them and deflected the blow. Dawson alone among the witnesses insinuated that Kate Dungey had felt nervous in the big house by herself, saying that she had told him she was afraid about a fortnight before her murder.

The coroner's jury deliberated for some time before returning a verdict that Miss Dungey was '...brutally murdered by some person or persons unknown'. It was announced at the end of the proceedings that Mr Mash had personally put up a reward of £100 for information leading to the arrest of the murderer(s) and, early in 1894, it looked as though that reward would soon be claimed, as the police arrested a suspect.

Twenty-four-year-old Walter Rathall was George Dawson's wife's brother and was married with a baby. He had previously worked for Mr Mash at Lambridge and was known to Kate Dungey, with whom he was said to be on friendly terms. Having inherited the sum of £100 from a relative, he had immediately given up working and instead lived off his inheritance.

For eight or nine weeks prior to the murder, Rathall and his wife and child had been staying at the Red Lion at Henley. James and Harry Froome had both seen Rathall in the immediate area of Lambridge on the day before the murder and, as a result, he was high on the list of people whom the police wanted to interview. However, when they went to try and talk to him at the Red Lion, he was out. Landlady Emily Ayres later told him that a policeman had come to see him about the murder and asked him directly if he had done it. 'No, Mrs Ayres,' replied Rathall. 'I could not hurt the poor creature.' The very next day, Rathall and his family hurriedly left the inn, owing money and without leaving a forwarding address.

A warrant was issued for Rathall's arrest and it was discovered that the family were in Daventry, Northamptonshire. Superintendent Keal sent a telegram to the Northamptonshire Constabulary, asking them to detain his fugitive and, although Rathall originally denied his true identity, telling the arresting officers that his name was John Browning, he was soon in custody. Keal immediately set off for Daventry to bring him back to Henley. Charged with Miss Dungey's murder, Rathall told Keal, 'You have got to prove it,' then refused to make any further comment on the matter, although during the train journey from Northampton to Henley, he was happy to chat about any other subject.

Rathall was met at Henley station by a welcoming committee comprising most of the residents of Henley. During the half-mile walk to the police station, he was loudly booed and heckled by the following crowd, who shouted suggestions of 'Lynch him!' to the four police officers escorting him. Rathall marched briskly on, his eyes fixed firmly to the front, somehow managing to ignore the hostile mob of people behind him, who were literally baying for his blood.

Walter Rathall appeared at a private sitting before magistrate Colonel Makins at Henley Police Court and was remanded in custody. He insisted that it was the police's job to prove that he had killed Kate Dungey, telling the magistrate that he had been in his lodgings all day on 8 December, apart from a brief trip into town between six o'clock and half past seven.

Rathall's next appearance before magistrates was on 11 January 1894, with solicitor Mr S. Brain of Reading prosecuting the case and Mr R.S. Wood acting for the defence.

Most of the witnesses who testified had already appeared at the inquest but there was one new piece of evidence. Frank Lillywhite was a pheasant farmer from Middle Assendon, which was between half and three quarters of a mile from Lambridge, as the crow flies. On the night of the murder, the wind was blowing from the direction of Lambridge Wood and, while he was visiting his pheasant pens at about 6.20 p.m., Lillywhite heard a fearful scream, which lasted for several seconds. If Lillywhite was correct in his timing and, if it had been Kate Dungey who had screamed, then the attack on her took place at a time when Rathall admitted to being out of his hotel.

Rathall was remanded for a week and the case resumed with evidence from surgeon George Smith and farm manager George Dawson. In questioning Dawson, the defence counsel made much of the argument during which Mrs Mash allegedly tried to hit Kate with an umbrella. The magistrates objected to the line of questioning, saying that they didn't think it was leading anywhere, at which Mr Wood said sharply, 'This is a case of suspicion and I am doing my best for my client. He is a poor man and if the other side has a right to impute grave matters to him, I am entitled to make imputations against others.'

Wood's response brought forth a smattering of enthusiastic applause, which was quickly quelled. Wood didn't pursue his 'imputations' any further after the magistrates stated that they didn't consider the story relating to Mr Mash as being of the slightest importance.

Continuing his cross-examination of Dawson, Wood established that, shortly before the murder, Kate Dungey had asked the farm manager to drive her to New Street in Henley and collect her on the following day. When he called back to pick her up as asked, he found that she had already left and had gone back to Lambridge without him. Dawson also told the magistrates that the police had left the house on the night of the murder, not returning until the next morning.

The chairman of the magistrates was incredulous. 'It passes my comprehension how the Superintendent could have allowed you to have anything to do with the house on the night of the murder and how it was he didn't leave a constable in charge,' he remarked, drawing another round of enthusiastic applause from the spectators.

No blood was ever found on any of Rathall's clothes. His boots had been taken from him on his arrest and, although they were similar in many respects to the plaster casts of the prints taken from Lambridge House, the soles of Rathall's

The Red Lion Hotel, Henley. (Author's collection)

hobnailed boots had a particularly individual pattern, which didn't match the prints at the scene of the crime.

There was, Mr Wood insisted, no real evidence to support the charge of wilful murder against his client and, after some debate, the magistrates agreed and Rathall was discharged, to yet more cheers from the public.

The identity of the murderer or murderers of Kate Dungey was never discovered and yet her untimely death raises some intriguing questions. What was the nature of the argument between Kate and Mrs Mash that so enraged her employer's wife that she was moved to physically attack the housekeeper with an umbrella? Could Mrs Mash have harboured suspicions about a possible affair between her husband and the attractive young servant he obviously held in such high esteem?

Why did Kate go to New Street only days before her murder, returning home earlier than she had intended, without even waiting for Dawson to collect her as previously arranged? Had she planned to meet somebody and, if so, did they quarrel, causing her to cut short her visit?

Both Mr Mash and Kate's father believed that staying alone in such a big house held no fears for the young woman. Yet, according to Dawson, only two weeks before her death she had told him that she felt nervous. Had something happened at the house to frighten her?

If he was innocent, why did Rathall flee the area so suddenly when he realised that the police were interested in talking to him about Kate's death?

And finally, what of George Dawson? He was known to have left work at the farm at about ten to five on the evening of the murder. However, he had left his home later that night, to fetch some beer for his wife and call on a neighbour. Remembering the Froomes' insistence that he had gone directly to Miss Dungey's body, could he have gone back to the house and killed Kate?

What was the motive for the murder? It seems most likely that somebody had planned to burgle the house and had possibly drugged the dog, which was known to bark at strangers. It seems probable that the housekeeper disturbed the would-be burglar or burglars, who were then forced to silence her – yet why use two different weapons, one blunt and one sharp? Could this indicate more than one attacker?

So long after the murder, such questions seem destined to remain unanswered.

Note: There are some discrepancies between different contemporary newspaper reports of the murder and its aftermath. For example, Miss Dungey's age is variously given as twenty-five and thirty years old and the number of her wounds varies between fifteen and twenty-four. I have used the most frequently cited 'facts' for this account.

19

'I CAN GO AND FACE THAT OUT'

Little Faringdon, 1893

On Saturday 22 July 1893, Henry Judd of Little Faringdon came home for his midday meal, which he ate with his wife, Mary, and the couple's five-year-old daughter Emily Ethel. Judd left to return to his work as a cowman and was gone until about five o'clock, when he came back home for his tea. Earlier that afternoon, Emily had gone out to play with a neighbour's child, seven-year-old Beatrice Alice James, and, when she didn't come home for tea, the Judds were not unduly worried, since their daughter had occasionally missed meals before when she was engrossed in playing with other children and lost track of the time. However, when Emily still hadn't arrived home by seven o'clock that evening, the Judds grew concerned – even more so when they found out that Beatrice was also missing.

Emily and Beatrice had been seen by several villagers at around a quarter past three that afternoon, walking towards Hookit's field, after which there had been no sign of them. A search was initiated immediately and people combed the area throughout the night but the search was to end in a tragic discovery at half past seven the next morning, when Henry Judd found his daughter's lifeless body in the River Leach, where it ran through a meadow known locally as The Steps.

Emily was floating in one of the deepest parts of the river, roughly 5ft away from the bank. The hat she had been wearing – a boy's cap – lay on the bank, about a yard from the water's edge. The dead child was pulled from the water and a surgeon was summoned from Lechlade. By the time Patrick Hunter Walker reached the scene at eleven o'clock that morning, *rigor mortis* had set in and Emily's body was quite stiff.

The surgeon estimated that she had been dead for at least twelve hours. There were no marks of violence whatsoever on the child's body and her hair was still neatly pinned up, exactly as it had been when she left home. Apart from having a small amount of froth around her nostrils, Emily looked as if she were sleeping peacefully rather than dead.

Even though Emily had now been found, there was still no sign of her companion, Beatrice, and the search continued. Since Emily had been found in the water, the searchers focused on dragging the river. Hence it wasn't until late the following morning that Beatrice's body was found in a dry ditch near to the river by gardener Phillip Batts.

Beatrice lay on her back in the ditch, her head tilted slightly to one side. Her legs were crossed and one arm was stretched out sideways, while the other was bent upwards towards her head. While Emily's body had been unmarked, the same could not be said for Beatrice, whose throat had been cut, leaving a deep, ragged wound that was crawling with maggots. She had heavy bruising to both of her thighs and, when her dress was lifted, a shallow, 4in cut was discovered, extending downwards from her navel. A few yards from where the child's body was found there was a depression in the grass, where a large quantity of her blood had formed a pool.

An inquest was opened into the death of the two little girls, at which the coroner, Mr F.J.D. Westell, explained that the two cases needed to be considered separately and that he proposed to begin by holding an inquest into the death of Emily Ethel Judd.

The jury having inspected both bodies, the inquest first heard from Mary Ann Turner, who had seen both girls passing her house in the village at 3.15 p.m. on Saturday. She had watched the girls walk towards the spot where their bodies were eventually found but could not say for certain whether they had turned off down the Lechlade road or continued straight on through the village.

Emily's father was next to give evidence, followed by the surgeon Mr Hunter Walker. The coroner then halted the proceedings, pointing out that there had been no formal post-mortem examination of Emily's body and telling the jury that it was up to them to decide whether or not they felt that one was needed.

The jury requested that a post-mortem examination was conducted and the inquest was adjourned for ninety minutes while Mr Hunter Walker honoured their request. When the inquest resumed, he was able to tell them that, in his opinion, Emily's death had been due to fright and had arisen from the sudden shock of hitting the cold water rather than as a result of drowning. Her lungs were full of air rather than water and there was just a small amount of frothy mucus in her windpipe.

Hunter Walker had found no marks of violence on Emily's body and concluded that she had not struggled once she was in the water. Having already examined the river banks close to where the child was found, he had seen no signs of any struggle or disturbance and no indication that Emily had slipped into the water. He therefore concluded that Emily had been thrown into the river, rather than falling in accidentally. Hunter Walker told the inquest that Emily's stomach contained a quantity of undigested potatoes and, when Henry Judd was recalled, he confirmed that his wife had served potatoes for their midday meal on the day his daughter disappeared. He could not be absolutely certain that Emily had eaten any but said that he knew that she was very fond of them.

With that, the coroner adjourned the inquest and opened the investigation into the death of Beatrice Alice James.

Mrs Turner repeated her evidence, after which Phillip Batts described finding the child's body in the dry ditch. The inquest next heard from Hunter Walker, who detailed Beatrice's injuries – a cut throat, a cut on her lower abdomen, which he believed had been made after her death, and severe bruising to both thighs. Attributing the cause of Beatrice's death to loss of blood from the severed arteries in her throat, Hunter Walker went on to say that he had examined the body with a microscope and discovered that an attempt had been made to rape Beatrice, although he was unable to determine if the attempt had been successful or not.

Beatrice's father, Isaac James, related his last sighting of his daughter and then Inspector Cooke, from Burford police station, told the inquest that there was already a suspect in custody and asked the coroner for more time to complete his enquiries. The inquest was duly adjourned until 2 August.

When the inquest resumed, the coroner announced that certain items thought to be connected to the murder of the two little girls had been sent to county analyst, Mr Walter William Fisher, who had not been able to complete his work in time to testify today. It was agreed that the inquest should be adjourned again to give him sufficient time to finish examining the artefacts in his possession. Inspector Cooke was then called to furnish the inquest with details about the suspect being held in custody in Oxford Prison.

Cooke stated that he had first been summoned to Little Faringdon after the discovery of the body of Beatrice James. After initial enquiries in the village, he discovered that a man named James Lapworth had been seen near to the field where her body had been found. Lapworth knew both girls and was actually godfather to one of the Judd's other children.

Cooke went straight to Lapworth's lodgings at Lechlade, intending to interview him, but Lapworth was not there and had not been to work that morning. The Inspector called in reinforcements and, together with Detective Sergeant Almond of the Oxfordshire police and Mr P.S. Hall of the Gloucestershire police, they began a search for the missing man, focusing on the Fairford and Lechlade areas.

At 4.15 a.m. on Tuesday 27 July, they reached the home of Lapworth's sister at Cerney Wick, where they found Lapworth asleep in bed. He was woken up and told to get dressed, at which point he was searched. Inspector Cooke told the inquest that two knives and a pair of scissors had been found in Lapworth's pockets, along with a heavily bloodstained handkerchief.

Cooke cautioned Lapworth before charging him with the murders of Emily Judd and Beatrice James. 'I can go and face that out,' said Lapworth, adding that he had not heard of the murders when he left Lechlade yesterday morning. The Inspector then took possession of all of Lapworth's clothes and, on 29 July, passed then to county analyst Mr Fisher for closer examination.

When the inquest resumed again, the jury's verdict was one of 'wilful murder' against twenty-seven-year-old James Lapworth. Mr Fisher testified to finding blood on the inside of the left sleeve of Lapworth's coat, with more blood on his waistcoat, trousers, shirt and handkerchief. It was Fisher's opinion that all of the bloodstains were relatively fresh, being between one and two weeks old. One of Lapworth's two knives was scratched, as if it had been recently cleaned and there was a small spot of fresh blood on the other.

Brought before a special sitting of magistrates at Burford Petty Sessions on 5 August, Lapworth had a ready explanation for the bloodstains on his clothes. He claimed that approximately three months earlier, he had tripped over a set of steps and bloodied his nose. William Deering, the landlord of the Temperance Hotel at Lechlade, testified to the fact that Lapworth had appeared at his premises with blood pouring from his nose and covering his hands and face. Lapworth, who was tipsy at the time, had told the landlord that he had fallen over Mr Eyles's step and broken his concertina. The magistrates chose to believe the analyst's testimony about the age of the bloodstains rather than Lapworth's and he was committed for trial at the next Oxford Assizes.

His case was prosecuted by Mr H.D. Greene QC and Mr Reginald Smith, while Mr Mackarness acted in Lapworth's defence. Initially, Lapworth was prosecuted only for the murder of Beatrice James, a charge to which he pleaded 'Not Guilty'.

The case for the prosecution was that the murder of Beatrice James had been carried out for lust, with an attempt made by her killer to violate the child either before or just after her death. Having established that a murder had been committed and suggesting the most probable motive, the counsel for the prosecution then told the jury that the next step was to determine who had committed the crime.

Mr Greene admitted that nobody had actually seen James Lapworth in the company of the two girls on the day of their disappearance. On the morning of 22 July, Lapworth was expected to work on a farm close to the scene of the crimes but, when he arrived for work in the morning, the weather had been too wet for him to carry out his job as a thatcher. Lapworth and the farmer had agreed to wait until the afternoon, to see if the weather improved and Lapworth had gone to the Swan public house at Southrop, where he had drunk three pints of ale and two of beer.

He left the pub at between one and two o'clock in the afternoon and walked off towards Little Faringdon. He had not been walking for long when he caught up with Mrs Elizabeth Stone and the two walked along together for some twenty-five minutes. Mrs Stone would later testify that Lapworth was tipsy at the time.

He and Mrs Stone parted at a farm lane, where Lapworth turned off, calling at the farm for some milk. The farmer, Philip Northcutt, testified that he had spoken to Lapworth at about one o'clock and he too stated that Lapworth had been 'the worse for drink' and, according to John Tanner, a young labourer at the farm, Lapworth was still on the land there at between two and three o'clock. Tanner also believed that Lapworth was drunk at the time.

Lapworth then went to Little Faringdon Mill, where, at between three o'clock and a quarter past three, he spoke to the owner's wife, Mrs Elizabeth Deacon, asking her if there was any work available. Told that there wasn't, he continued to walk towards the village.

Carpenter George James Brown was the next witness to see Lapworth at about 3.45 p.m. on the day of the murders. By then, Lapworth was sitting on the rails by the gate to Hookit's field. Brown said, 'How do, Jemmy,' to Lapworth, who responded with a similar remark. However, fishmonger William Stevens was next to take the witness stand and he testified that Brown had been at his house at around the time when he purported to have seen Lapworth at Hookit's field gate.

However, another man, furniture dealer Charles Smart, saw Lapworth sitting on the rails at about the same time, when the two men exchanged pleasantries about the weather. Ten minutes later, Lapworth was still in the same place, according to witness William Lapworth (no relation). From then, Lapworth was seen near the gate of Lord de Mauley's lodge house, then on the road to Lechlade.

By 6.15 p.m., he was in the Railway Tavern at Lechlade, where he was described by witness Henry Edwards as looking 'rather wild about the eyes, as if he had been crying'. Someone had come into the pub shortly afterwards, asking if anyone had seen anything of the two missing girls, at which Lapworth almost immediately stood up and said that he must be going. Although Lapworth was within 3ft of the conversation about the missing girls, under cross-examination by the defence, those witnesses who had been in the pub at the time admitted that there had been a bit of 'larking about' going on and that they couldn't be absolutely positive that Lapworth had heard the remarks about the missing children.

Sarah Search, Lapworth's landlady, stated that her lodger had arrived home at about eleven o'clock on the night of the murder. On the following day, he had been out for a walk, although he had eaten his meals at her home then, on the Monday, he had gone off to his sister's house without telling her that he was going. Cross-examined by the counsel for the defence, Mrs Search admitted that Lapworth had gone to his sister's on previous occasions without telling her. She also testified that she had seen her lodger using his knife to make picture frames and that, in doing so, he often cut his fingers. She added that Lapworth frequently suffered from nosebleeds.

Once Lapworth's movements on the day of the murder had been established, the prosecution called analyst Mr Fisher. Having given his qualifications and told the court that he was a Fellow of the Institute of Chemistry, Fisher went on to describe the testing of the garments and knives presented to him by Inspector Cooke.

Fisher had found a smear of blood on the inside of one of Lapworth's coat sleeves, as well as numerous spots and smears of blood on his waistcoat, trousers and shirt. There was also blood on the edge of the blade of one of the knives, although Fisher could not definitely determine whether that blood was human or animal.

The blood on the knife was the freshest sample, being the brightest in colour. Fisher believed that all of the stains were of recent origin and that, at the time of his examination, they were consistent with stains acquired on 22 July.

Following Mr Fisher's evidence, the prosecution rested and Mr Mackarness opened his case for the defence. His first witness was Mr Deering of the Temperance Hotel in Lechlade, who repeated his testimony from the magistrates' court in relation to seeing Lapworth covered in blood, following his alleged fall on Mr Eyles's steps. Mackarness also called Mary Adams, servant to Mr Eyles, who testified to finding a considerable quantity of blood on the steps at the end of April that year.

Next to testify was labourer William Newport, who had been working in the area where the bodies of the two girls were found on the day of their murders until four o'clock in the afternoon. He stated that he had neither seen nor heard the girls and neither had he seen Lapworth in the area. John and Thomas Cox, who had been working with Newport, said exactly the same.

The defence next called Mr Marcus S. Pembrey, a Bachelor of Medicine and university lecturer. Pembrey had examined Lapworth's clothes and said that, in his opinion, it was simply not possible to determine the age of the bloodstains on them. Furthermore, the bloodstains on the handkerchief took the form of round, clearly defined spots and bore no resemblance to the stains he would have expected to have been made by blood spurting from an artery.

There was a smattering of applause from the spectators in the court at this time, at which the judge threatened to clear the court if there was any repetition.

Under cross-examination by the counsel for the prosecution, Pembrey admitted that he held no office as an analyst and had never practised as one. However, it was his opinion that Mr Fisher had used the wrong tests in examining the bloodstains and Pembrey stuck firmly to his belief that it was impossible to accurately estimate the age of a bloodstain once it was more than one day old.

Pembrey was followed into the witness box by Dr Drew FRCS, who had also examined the clothing. He agreed with Pembrey that it simply wasn't possible to give the age of bloodstains. In his opinion, the marks on the coat and shirt were consistent with bleeding from scratched flea bites, while that on the handkerchief had most probably been the result of a nosebleed. None of the stains he had seen were consistent with arterial bleeding.

A third medical witness, Dr Brooks from the Radcliffe Infirmary, concurred with Pembrey and Drew.

The defence then called a series of character witnesses for the defendant, who was variously described as 'quiet', 'inoffensive' and 'a good worker'.

Mr Mackarness then addressed the jury for the defence. He pointed out that the prosecution had the financial resources to be able to present the strongest, most forcible case possible against the prisoner whereas, until three or four days ago,

Lapworth had been without any defence at all and was only now defended due to the charity of friends who strongly believed in his innocence.

Mackarness then went on to discuss the terrible nature of the crime against two innocent little girls, saying that, in his experience, '... the horrible incidents of the case were unparalleled' and that he never remembered anything so wicked and so terrible.

'Where was the man who was capable of committing such acts?' he asked the jury. It was only natural to assume that such a man would have travelled from one crime to the next and put the climax on his career of iniquity by perpetrating this horrible atrocity.

The man in the dock was not a gaol bird who was crowning a long career of crime but a young man who had spent the whole of his life in a quiet, secluded village. There was nothing in his past that could suggest even the slightest criminal intent or any disposition that would make it possible for him to commit such a crime as this.

'Who are the victims?' Mackarness continued. They were two little children, the daughters of neighbours, who Lapworth had lived close to for the whole of his life. He was on friendly terms with both families, so much so that he was godfather to one of the Judds' children.

Lapworth had not been seen with the girls on that fateful day – indeed, nobody had been able to place him closer than half or three-quarters of a mile to the children at any time.

Medical evidence had suggested that one of the girls died within three hours of eating her last meal, which would place the time of her death at around 3.30 p.m. Fifteen minutes earlier Lapworth had been at Little Faringdon Mill, asking for work. Lapworth knew every inch of that village and he also knew that, around the time that he was supposed to have been murdering the children, men would be leaving work and walking home. Indeed, there had been workmen in the immediate area at around the time that the murders allegedly took place and not one of them had heard so much as a whimper, never mind any screams.

Could it be possible that Lapworth would be capable of sitting on a gate appearing quite normal, able to exchange pleasantries with passers-by so soon after brutally murdering two young children? Was it conceivable that any man, however debased he might be, could act in such a nonchalant way immediately after committing two such horrible killings?

Mr Fisher had given his evidence with extreme fairness and candour. Yet his evidence had been merely an opinion and the defence had found no less than three eminent witnesses who disagreed with that opinion. The very moment that the bloodstains were brought to Lapworth's attention, he had produced a credible explanation for their presence, one which had later been corroborated by other witnesses.

Fisher's investigations had destroyed much of the bloodstain evidence on Lapworth's clothes and the defence had only a very hurried opportunity to examine the clothes after his tests had been carried out. The defence could not disprove Fisher's testimony but believed that the matter of the bloodstains now rested with whichever expert on the subject the jury found most credible.

As for the blood on the knife, it had been found on the smaller of the two knives in Lapworth's possession and the doctors who had conducted Beatrice's post-mortem examination believed that knife to have been too small to cause her terrible injuries. It was far more likely that the blood came from cuts on Lapworth's hands, obtained while he was making picture frames.

The defence closed by reminding the jury that it was not up to the defence to prove Lapworth innocent but for the prosecution to prove him guilty. If they convicted Lapworth purely on the basis of circumstantial evidence, then the punishment he stood to receive could never be undone.

Replying on behalf of the prosecution, Mr Greene maintained that circumstantial evidence was no less satisfactory than any other kind. Saying that the prosecution had no wish to prove an innocent man guilty, he added that there was a whole hour of time on the afternoon of the murders during which Lapworth's whereabouts could not be accounted for. Nobody but Lapworth had been seen in the area and, being close to a river, he would have had ample time to wash his hands and his knives after killing Beatrice.

With regard to the bloodstain evidence, the prosecution believed that Mr Fisher had conducted his tests fairly and diligently and come up with the correct results. Greene reminded the jury that blood had been found on Lapworth's shirt, which, according to his landlady, had been recently washed before Lapworth put it on, on the Wednesday before the murders. The blood on the shirt could not have come from a fall three months earlier.

In his summary of the evidence for the jury, his Lordship cautioned them against allowing their natural revulsion against the perpetrator of such horrible atrocities to colour their consideration of the evidence that had been presented in court. The judge went over the various timings very carefully. Going by the evidence of Emily's stomach contents, he judged the time of her death to be around half past three in the afternoon. The two girls had been seen together in the village fifteen minutes earlier and another witness, Mrs Betts, had walked the same route roughly five minutes before the girls and had seen nothing.

This left a scant quarter of an hour for the girls to get from where they were last seen alive to the place where Emily's body was found, assuming the time of death determined by the doctor to have been accurate. If they had been met or overtaken by some man who had then attacked them, how had he managed to control both girls at once? It would be more logical to assume that one girl briefly got away while he was dealing with her friend and, if this was indeed the case, then it was likely that she would have screamed. Even if the man had quickly dealt with Emily by throwing her into the river, leaving him free to concentrate on Beatrice, why had Beatrice not screamed or called for help? The fact that the men working nearby in the fields had seen or heard nothing seemed remarkable.

Lapworth left Little Faringdon Mill at 3.15 p.m., from there it was a five minute walk to Hookit's field. Witnesses had seen him sitting on rails by the gate at 3.45 p.m., which gave him a mere twenty-five minutes to go down the path after the children, overtake them, throw one girl into the river, take the other girl a distance of 1,000 yards, rape her, kill her, dispose of her body, wash his hands and his knife and get back to the rails by Hookit's gate. That would, said the judge, be extremely sharp work, although not absolutely impossible. Nevertheless, the mere fact that the defendant could have committed the murders didn't necessarily mean that he had done so and there was a great deal of difference between possibility and probability.

Lapworth had undoubtedly been in the area at the time, having done what many men before him had done – he had had a few too many drinks in the pub that morning. There was nothing to suggest that he was so befuddled by drink as to be unaware of what he was doing.

Numerous people had supplied the defendant with excellent character references, making it difficult to believe that he had suddenly changed into the type of perfect fiend who could destroy these children so brutally and barbarically. Dealing with the scientific evidence, the judge pointed out that, in a case of life or death, such as this one, it was only fair to expect the scientific experts to agree in their conclusions. There were three witnesses in favour of the defendant and just one against him and the judge said that he would leave the jury to decide which of the experts' opinions they found most believable.

At the conclusion of the judge's summary, the jury retired for a mere three minutes before returning to pronounce Lapworth 'Not Guilty' of the wilful murder of Beatrice James. Lapworth was then charged on the second indictment, that of the murder of Emily Ethel Judd.

Mr Greene informed the court that the prosecution would not be offering any evidence relating to that charge, leaving the judge to discharge the prisoner against a background of fervent applause from the spectators.

Having left the dock, where he had been sitting calmly for the entire eight hour duration of the trial, Lapworth went with some relatives to a café in Castle Street for refreshments. A crowd of several hundred people surrounded the café hoping to get a glimpse of him and later followed him *en masse* as he was driven by cab to the railway station for his journey home.

Following Lapworth's acquittal, this author has been unable to find any evidence to suggest that anyone else was ever charged with the murders of Beatrice Alice James and Emily Ethel Judd, so can only assume that the crime remains unsolved.

Note: In some contemporary accounts of the murders, Beatrice Alice James is referred to as Alice Beatrice James. Official records seem to support the former version of her name.

20

'POLICE OFFICERS DO NOT WEAR A HALO AND DO NOT ALWAYS SPEAK THE TRUTH'

Gallows Tree Common, near Henley-on-Thames, 1922

Sarah Blake and her husband were the licensees of the Crown and Anchor public house at Gallows Tree Common, near Henley-on-Thames, until Mr Blake died in 1921. Fifty-year-old Sarah decided to apply for the licence to be transferred to her name only and, by March 1922, was on the verge of appearing at the Petty Sessions for the consideration of her application.

Gallows Tree Common was very secluded and there were only thirty-five houses in the area. It was the kind of place where everyone knew everyone else, yet Sarah Blake was a very private person, who tended to keep herself to herself. She had just one close friend – her next-door neighbour, Mrs Ellen Elizabeth Payne.

On 4 March, Sarah Blake found herself obliged to take a short business trip and her friend Ellen willingly agreed to take over the running of the pub in her absence. Ellen went to the Crown and Anchor in the morning to receive any last minute instructions and, to her surprise she found the front door of the inn still locked. Ellen knocked and called for Mrs Blake for some time but was unable to get any response. Growing ever more concerned, she decided to force the door and, when she finally managed to get into the pub, she walked into an unbelievable scene of carnage.

Sarah Blake lay dead on the kitchen floor in a pool of blood, which had splattered liberally around the walls of the pub. Broken glass littered the area around Sarah's body. Her hair hung down around her face and every inch of her flesh was plastered in gore. A later post-mortem examination, carried out by Home Office pathologist Sir Bernard Spilsbury and Dr Luff from St Mary's Hospital, showed that Sarah had suffered more than sixty wounds to her head, hands, face, neck and left arm. She had clearly put up a tremendous fight against whoever had attacked her. Her skull was fractured in four places, her right ear was almost torn from the side of her head and one cheekbone was broken, with other serious injuries to her jaw and neck. One neck wound in particular was more than a simple stab wound and, according to Spilsbury, looked as though someone had plunged a knife into Mrs Blake's neck and then 'worked it about'.

The first policeman to arrive in response to Ellen's call was PC Buswell, who began a search of the premises. He noticed that there were two glasses on the bar, one containing mineral water and the other half full of beer. Although the inn appeared to have been ransacked, Buswell found a bowl and a biscuit tin in the pub kitchen, between them containing almost £10. More than £250 was found in the bedroom, along with a bank book with a balance of £465 and a Treasury bond. Ellen Payne was able to tell Buswell that the bowl containing the money was normally kept in the pub cellar, where Buswell found yet more bloodstains. Most significant of all were bloody fingerprints in the cellar and on the inside of the front door.

The police enquiries soon covered every house in the hamlet and they quickly came to the conclusion that the murderer or murderers most probably came from outside the area. Sarah Blake had last been seen alive at six o'clock on the evening of 3 March 1922 and it was estimated that she had been killed within two hours of that last sighting. Having eliminated those living near to the pub as suspects and aware that anyone leaving the scene of the crime and heading towards nearby Reading would have had immediate rail access to almost anywhere in the country, Superintendent Wastie of the Oxfordshire Constabulary telephoned Scotland Yard and Detective Inspector Helden and Superintendent Ryan were sent to assist the local police.

Although money and valuables had been found at the pub and there was little evidence that much had been stolen, the police were working on the theory that the motive for the murder could have been robbery. The two half-empty glasses left on the bar seemed to suggest the presence of two men and, as the front door of the pub had been locked from the inside, and the killer(s) had left by the back door, it was thought that whoever killed Mrs Blake may have been familiar with the internal layout of the premises. The police appealed in the local newspapers for a cyclist, seen entering the pub at the crucial time, to come forward.

They had so far traced only two people who had visited the pub on the night of the murder. The first of these was a fifteen-year-old local boy named Jack Hewitt, who had called in for a glass of 'raspberry champagne' and a bottle of ginger stout.

Hewitt told the police that he had been at the pub for only a few minutes and that, while he was there, Ellen Payne's husband had come in for a beer and that he too had not stayed long.

The police began a search of the immediate area and, within days of the murder, made some significant finds. These included the bloodstained key to the front door of the pub, which seemingly materialised in plain view on a patch of grass in front of the building hours after the area had been carefully searched.

The next find was an empty calico bag, identical to those in which Mrs Blake kept the pub takings, which was found in a nearby wood. Then, on 14 March, the police found a rusted, open clasp knife in a hedge about 30 yards from the pub. The knife bore what looked like bloodstains and several long hairs were stuck to the blade, which were of a similar colour and texture to the victim's hair. When the knife was shown to Spilsbury, he agreed that it could have caused some of Mrs Blake's wounds.

Soon after finding the probable murder weapon, the police had a suspect in custody. Robert Alfred Sheppard, a twenty-four-year-old woodcutter from Reading, was arrested on 15 March for an unrelated burglary charge. At Reading police station he asked to see Detective Sergeant Henderson, telling him that he wanted to talk about 'that stunt on Friday night.'

Cautioned by the policeman, Sheppard made a voluntary statement, in which he said that he had been drinking in Henley on the day of the murder, with a man he knew only as Jack Larking. Sheppard's companion told him that he knew of a place where they could get some money, offering to split the proceeds with him if Sheppard would act as his lookout. The two men then walked until they came to a pub and, while Larking went in, Sheppard stood guard outside, ready to alert him if anyone came by. Sheppard told the police that, while waiting, he spoke to a passing cyclist, asking him the time, and was told that it was five minutes to ten. Describing Larking as being between thirty and thirty-five years old and having dark hair, Sheppard continued to say that Larking had never returned and he had not seen him since.

Knowing about the murder in the neighbouring county, Detective Sergeant Henderson sent a message to Superintendent Wastie, who arrived in Reading with Inspector Helden later that day, bringing with him the knife. Sheppard was visibly shaken when he saw it.

'Look here, what shall I get for the burglary?' he asked, adding, 'I want to say something else. Give me a drop of water first.'

As Henderson rose to fetch him some water, Sheppard suddenly snatched up the statement he had just dictated from the desk. 'I did do the murder,' he said as he ripped up his statement and threw the pieces on the floor. 'I had a bicycle, which was a pinched one. It was earlier in the evening than I told you.' Sheppard went on to dictate a second statement, in which he admitted sole responsibility for the murder of Sarah Blake. When Helden examined the coat that Sheppard was wearing, he noticed what looked like bloodstains on the lining. 'I wiped them over since,' Sheppard remarked.

Sheppard was taken before magistrates at Reading Police Court on 17 March, charged with burglary. The police offered no evidence and requested Sheppard's discharge, which was granted. On his release, Sheppard was promptly arrested by Inspector Helden and charged with the wilful murder of Mrs Blake.

An inquest had been opened into Mrs Blake's death and adjourned. By the time it resumed on 21 March, Sheppard had changed his story and was insisting that the police had forced a confession from him. As Detective Sergeant Henderson told the inquest about Sheppard's request to see him, Sheppard angrily shouted at him to 'Keep to the truth, Sergeant.'

Henderson went on to discuss Sheppard's second statement, after which Sheppard asked the coroner if he might question the policeman.

'Did I sign the second statement?' he asked.

'Yes,' replied Henderson.

'Why did I sign it?'

'I read it over to you and asked if you wished to add anything to it.'

'Did you say that if I signed the form there would be no need for you to go and search my home?'

'No. I did not wish to search your home.'

'Have you spoken all the truth?'

'Certainly I have,' Henderson assured him.

'That's enough for me. You are a lying hound,' Sheppard accused him.

His outburst got him nowhere and he was summoned to appear before magistrates at Caversham on 7 April, charged on his own confession. However, at that appearance he was immediately released, although he was quickly arrested again on a charge of burglary at Reading. Once Sheppard had been officially discharged, another person took his place at the magistrates' court and Jack Hewitt was then charged with the wilful murder of Mrs Blake.

With Sheppard safely in custody for the murder, the police had received information that Jack Hewitt had been seen peering intently into the hedge where the knife had been found. As he was known to have been in the pub on the night of the murder, Hewitt was interviewed again after 14 March and shown the knife, denying ever having owned a similar one. Hewitt, who lived within 200 yards of the Crown and Anchor, worked as a labourer on a farm owned by Mr Paddick and, when Paddick's foreman, Joseph Haines, was routinely interviewed on 4 April, he stated that he believed the knife to be Hewitt's. Haines was completely certain in his identification of the knife, since he had borrowed it from the boy during February.

The police went straight to Hewitt's place of work, finding him in a stable, and questioned him again about ownership of the knife. Although Hewitt continued to deny that the knife was his, he was to spend more than five hours in the stable with the police and, by the time the interview terminated, Superintendent Wastie had a signed confession.

Hewitt told the police that he had been in the pub at about six o'clock on the evening of the murder. Mr Payne had come in for a beer and left soon afterwards.

Alone in the pub with the landlady, Hewitt said he picked up a piece of iron and struck her with it. There had been a fierce struggle, during which he had stabbed Mrs Blake with the knife, which he now admitted was his. He then locked the front door and went home, throwing the key down in the garden and disposing of the knife in the hedge. Hewitt admitted, 'I don't know what made me strike Mrs Blake but when I struck her I could not stop.'

Hewitt was committed for trial at the next Oxford Assizes and appeared before Mr Justice Shearman on 2 June 1922, with Mr J.B. Matthews and Mr G. Milward prosecuting. Hewitt, who was defended by Mr Thomas Gates and Mr A.E. Godson, pleaded 'Not Guilty' to the charge of wilful murder against him. His defence was paid for by a wealthy and philanthropic countess, who read about the case in the newspaper and contacted Hewitt's parents offering financial assistance.

In the course of the trial Hewitt took the stand and gave an account of his movements on the night of the murder. He told the court that a naturalist had given him a shilling for finding two squirrels' nests and he decided to call in at the pub to spend some of his money. He bought a 'raspberry champagne' and a ginger stout, for which he paid 3*d*.

Mrs Blake was alone at the pub when he arrived but Mr Payne had come in very shortly afterwards and drunk some beer. Hewitt said that he had followed Mr Payne out of the pub and gone from there to Mr Smith's shop, which served as a meeting place for the young people of the village. On the way to Smith's, Hewitt said that he had met his mother.

After hanging around aimlessly at Smith's for an hour and twenty minutes, Hewitt told the court that he went home. When he got there, his mother sent him back to the Crown and Anchor to fetch some beer, but the pub was in darkness when he arrived and he had assumed that Mrs Blake had closed up and gone to bed.

Hewitt again denied that the knife found in the hedge belonged to him, saying that he didn't have a knife on him at all on the night of the murder, having lent his to his father on the previous evening. Questioned further, Hewitt told the court that he had sold the knife that he lent to Joseph Haines shortly before the murder, although he couldn't recall who he sold it to, how much he got for it or where the sale had taken place. He admitted that marks resembling bloodstains had been found on his clothing but pointed out that he often killed rabbits or chickens.

Asked why he had signed a confession, Hewitt insisted that he had never even read it. He alleged that Wastie had written something down in his notebook and told him that, if he didn't sign it, he would be locked up. Hewitt appeared to believe that if he signed his name to what was written in the notebook, he would be allowed to go home.

Instead he was taken to Caversham police station and questioned by PC Buswell, who asked him what he had done with the piece of iron. Hewitt denied ever having had a piece of iron. Hewitt told the court that he had never been cautioned, nor had the police read the statement he was supposed to have made back to him. They had just handed him a pencil and told him to sign the notebook page.

'I have never struck Mrs Blake,' he insisted to the court.

Mr Matthews addressed the court for the prosecution, saying that if the story Hewitt was now telling was true, '... the police administration of the whole affair would be infamy too black for description.' Could the jury really believe that all four officers involved had committed such terrible perjury?

Matthews drew the jury's attention to the alleged sale of the knife, asking them if it were possible that Hewitt had sold the knife and yet been unable to recall who he had sold it to, how much he had got for it and even where he was when the deal took place? The sale of the knife was a cock and bull story, invented by Hewitt to deny ownership of the murder weapon.

Mr Gates, for the defence, told the jury, 'Police officers do not wear a halo and do not always speak the truth.' He asked them to consider why Hewitt would have signed a confession if no inducement had been offered for him to do so.

A confession should not be used against a person unless it was made properly without any improper influence. To call this confession voluntary was a mockery, since the police had played a cat and mouse game with the defendant and had not arrested him because, had they done so, they would not have been able to question him. Gates suggested that this was a case of Scotland Yard versus the local constabulary and that there was a good deal of jealousy between the two parties, resulting in a desire to secure a conviction, regardless of the facts.

Where was the cyclist, who had been seen by several witnesses to enter the pub at half past seven? Why had he never come forward? And where was the iron bar, with which the defendant was alleged to have struck Mrs Blake and which had never been found?

In his summary of the evidence, Mr Justice Shearman told them that it was not unusual for so young a boy to commit such a crime. 'Quite young boys show murderous instincts,' stated the judge, adding that, if convicted, Hewitt was too young for the death penalty to apply. The crux of the defence case was that four police officers had committed perjury here in court and had fabricated a story in order to obtain a conviction. The jury must decide if they believed that such a thing could have happened.

The jury deliberated the case during the luncheon interval, returning to pronounce Jack Hewitt 'Guilty'. In view of his age, he was ordered by the judge to be detained during the King's pleasure.

Note: There are some minor discrepancies in contemporary accounts of the murder, with some newspapers stating that Ellen Payne initially broke into the pub and others reporting the first entrant to have been PC Buswell. Helden, the officer from Scotland Yard, is referred to as both Detective Inspector and Chief Inspector and his name is variously spelled Heldon and Helden.

21

'I HAVE COMMITTED A MURDER TONIGHT'

Noke, 1927

At about half past ten on the night of 26 January 1927, a pleasant-faced young man with blond hair and a fresh, pink complexion arrived at the county police station at Oxford and rang the doorbell. When PC Robert Seeley Wingrove answered the door, the man asked to speak to the Superintendent.

'What do you want him for?' asked the constable.

'I would rather tell him than you,' replied the young man cryptically.

Wingrove took the man's name and address and asked him again what his business with the Superintendent was.

'Murder,' responded the man, who had given his name as Frederick Boxall and told the constable that he was a cowman at Lower Hall Farm in Noke. He had walked almost 9 miles from his place of employment to the police station.

Boxall was ushered into the office of Superintendent Francis Day, who asked what he could do for him.

'I have committed a murder tonight,' the young man calmly told the astounded police officer. 'I have choked a girl and left her under the hedge at Noke.'

Once Superintendent Day had recovered his composure, he quickly cautioned Boxall and took a statement from him, noticing as he did that there was fresh blood on Boxall's shirt, along with a couple of superficial scratches on his jaw.

Nineteen-year-old Boxall told Day that he had arranged to meet fifteen-year-old Katherine Mary Baker, whom he called Molly, that night. Molly was the niece of his employers, Mr and Mrs Franklin. She was the daughter of William Baker, who owned the Stag Hunters Hotel near Barnstaple in Devon, and had been living with

The Stag Hunters Hotel, Brendon, near Barnstaple, Devon. (Author's collection)

the Franklins at Lower Farm in Noke for just over a year. 'We had a quarrel just outside the farm.' Boxall continued:

> I do not know what happened next. I took her by the throat. She fell down in the road and I picked her up and carried her along the road. Then I fell over with her, still carrying her. I put her behind the hedge and left her lying there. Then I came to Oxford and asked for Superintendent Day at the county police station.

Having taken a statement from the self-confessed murderer, Day then called in the police surgeon, Dr Richard Sankey, and a colleague, Detective Inspector Edwin J. Rippington, and together they drove Boxall back to Noke, where he obligingly pointed out the location of the body.

The young woman lay on her back, her dress wet and mud-stained and her collar over her mouth. A handkerchief was wound loosely around her neck, knotted twice. Although dead, her body was still warm and Dr Sankey estimated that she had been dead for between four and five hours. When Sankey conducted a post-mortem examination, he found the marks of a ligature around her throat and a bruise on her temple, which could have been caused by either a fall or a blow and might have rendered her unconscious.

Apart from these injuries, other than a few small scratches on the dead girl's face and a small bruise on her lip, she had no other marks anywhere on her body and did not appear to have been sexually assaulted. Sankey determined the cause of death to be strangulation by ligature, theorising that the handkerchief loosely knotted around her neck had been tightly pulled or twisted from behind. However, Sankey also found that Molly's thymus gland was enlarged; a condition that he believed might have made her more susceptible to a condition known as status lymphaticus or sudden death.

Noke, the village where Katherine Mary Baker was murdered (© N. Sly)

Molly had already been reported missing by the time the police called on her aunt and uncle to tell them the tragic news of her murder and her uncle had been out searching the village for her. For some months she had been taking evening classes at the home of the village schoolmistress, Miss Melina Bartlett, usually attending three evenings every week and staying for about an hour and a half each time. As far as her aunt and uncle were aware, that was where she had been that evening. Her attendance was later confirmed by Miss Bartlett, although she told the police that Molly had been a bit late arriving and consequently had left a little later than normal. Neither Mr nor Mrs Franklin knew of any relationship between their niece and their cowman and Mr Franklin insisted that, had he been aware of any friendship between them, he would have nipped it in the bud immediately. However, a search of Boxall's room at the farm told a very different story.

The police found Boxall's diary, with entries dating from 1 January to the day before the murder.

Jan 1: Molly let me nurse her and seemed quite friendly.

Jan 2: Went back to the old style. Molly in a temper. Turned her back on me when I spoke to her.

Jan 7: I miss Molly very much.

Jan 8: Very slow and feeling fed up. Miss teasing her very much.

Jan 11: One month ago today Molly kissed me. I wish she would kiss me every day.

Jan 16: Molly in a temper with a face as long as a wet week. Wanted to kiss her but she wouldn't let me.

Jan 17: Resolved not to speak to Molly again until she is more friendly.

Jan 18: Molly pinched my photos and will not give them back.

Jan 20: Molly still refuses to give up my photos, so I boned her watch.

Jan 21: Gave Molly her watch back. She promised to give me my photos back.

Jan 22: Molly is in no hurry to keep her promise to give me my photos. Molly gave me a note asking me to give her the photos. I do not know what to do.

Jan 23: Told her to keep photos but I wanted a kiss or else would not speak to her again.

Jan 24: Molly would not kiss me and would not speak. She tried to take her keepsake from me but I got it back.

Jan 26: Feeling fed up. Molly does not care, so now know she does not love me but has only been playing with me. I wish I were dead.

With the diary were a number of short, handwritten verses, some initialled F.B., others K.M.B. The police also found a mineral water bottle filled with a solution of verdigris and a packet labelled 'Verdigris – Poison'. Verdigris was used as a treatment for foot rot in animals and, when Boxall was asked about its presence in his room, he told the police that he had intended to use it to poison himself after quarrelling with Molly after Christmas 1926.

Brought before magistrates, charged with Molly's murder, Boxall waited until minutes before his hearing was due to start to ask if he might make another statement, saying, 'What I told you on 26 January is not all true'. Now he told the police that he had been having 'certain relations' with Molly and that Molly had been intending to tell her uncle. Boxall had asked her not to and the couple had quarrelled. According to Boxall, Molly had smacked him in the mouth and he had retaliated by pushing her. It then entered his mind to kill her so that she could not tell her uncle about their relationship. It seems that Molly believed she was pregnant and was on the verge of confessing all to her uncle, even though Boxall pleaded with her to wait for a while before doing so, doubtless keen to ensure that the pregnancy scare was not just a false alarm.

Boxall refused to give evidence at his hearing. 'I've nothing to say,' he commented tersely when given the opportunity to speak. The magistrates committed him for trial at the next assizes and Boxall was asked if he would prefer to be tried at Oxford or Birmingham. 'The sooner, the better,' he replied.

In the event, his trial took place at the Oxford Assizes before Mr Justice Greer. Mr J.B. Matthews KC prosecuted the case with the assistance of Mr Morrison. Boxall, who now pleaded 'Not Guilty', was defended by Mr Ralph Thomas.

Between the magistrates' hearing and the trial, the police had requested another post-mortem examination, which had been carried out by Home Office pathologist Sir Bernard Spilsbury. Spilsbury had supervised the exhumation of Miss Baker's body on 12 February and his findings had largely concurred with those of Dr Sankey. Like Sankey, Spilsbury noted Molly's enlarged thymus gland, although Spilsbury did not believe that this would make Molly more likely to suffer from status lymphaticus. He also confirmed that the girl was not pregnant. The cause of her death was asphyxia or suffocation, consistent with strangulation, and it was Spilsbury's opinion that whoever strangled her would have needed to keep up the pressure on her throat for an absolute minimum of three minutes and, more probably, at least five minutes in order to kill her.

Boxall was now prepared to speak in his own defence. He told the court that he had been terrified at the thought that Molly was intending to tell her uncle about her condition that day. 'That was the first moment that I had any idea of killing her,' he said. He described how he seized Molly by the throat and she instantly fell down, giving 'a little twitch'. Boxall thought that she had fainted until he took hold of her wrist and realised that he couldn't feel her pulse. He had picked Molly up and blood had run from her mouth, so he had wrapped his handkerchief around her mouth to stop the blood from running out. He had carried her for a while, then left her and sat on a wall for some time wondering what he should do. Thinking it would be best to go to the police, he set off on the long walk to Oxford. 'I did not mean to kill her. I meant to frighten more than anything,' he explained. 'It did not seem like three minutes while I held her throat. I was in a temper and excited and I did not take any notice of the time.'

Mr Thomas summarised the case for the defence admitting that he could not, in all honesty, ask the jury to find his client 'Not Guilty' of any offence. However, he pointed out that insanity had been found in Boxall's family and, although Boxall himself showed no overt signs of it, he was, according to both Sir Bernard Spilsbury and Dr Sankey, at the dangerous age of between seventeen and twenty-three when hereditary insanity was most likely to develop. Spilsbury went further, saying that Boxall's conduct after the murder was consistent with that of a person suffering from homicidal mania.

Boxall's diary showed his state of extreme depression at the time of the murder. Had Boxall carried out his intention to commit suicide, no jury would have failed to return a verdict of suicide due to temporary insanity. The diaries also showed something else – that Boxall was desperately in love with Molly. It was almost impossible to believe that Boxall was sufficiently callous and brutal as to slowly strangle the girl he loved to such an extent.

Thomas suggested to the jury that the prosecution's theory that Molly was strangled with the handkerchief was untenable. It was hard to imagine how Boxall could have put the handkerchief around Molly's throat while she was standing up and, if she had been strangled from behind as the prosecution maintained, then she could not have been lying on the ground at the time since no mud was found on the front of her dress. Molly's death was far more likely to have been as Boxall had testified, her enlarged thymus gland causing her to suddenly collapse when Boxall had grasped her throat to try and frighten her.

Mr Matthews addressed the court for the prosecution, reminding them that three minutes was a very long time for a man to tightly grasp the throat of a young woman, who must have struggled to try and free herself from the terrible attack against her. The defence had called no evidence to suggest that Boxall was not responsible for the deed, said Matthews, although he admitted that Boxall had a great uncle who had spent many years in an asylum. However, Dr Watson, the senior medical officer for Brixton Prison, where Boxall had been incarcerated since the murder, had observed the prisoner constantly throughout his time in custody. He had found Boxall to be completely healthy physically and of above average intelligence. Watson had detected no signs of any insanity or mental abnormality whatsoever and regarded the insanity of Boxall's great uncle as practically irrelevant.

It was left to the judge to summarise the evidence for the jury. Mr Justice Greer stated that, if it were proved that an accused person killed another then that was murder, unless there was something in the circumstances that could reduce it to either justifiable homicide or manslaughter. After hearing the evidence presented in court, Greer told the jury that he did not think that they could have any doubts that the defendant killed the girl. He reminded the jury that even if the act committed by the prisoner had only accelerated the victim's death, it was still murder – it didn't matter whether or not she had a disease that might render her more liable to death.

The defence had argued that the evidence suggested that this was a case of manslaughter – an act committed in hot blood – and that, regardless of whether it was murder or manslaughter, it was the act of a man who was insane at the time. If the prisoner intended to kill his victim or to do her grievous bodily harm then it was murder and the prisoner's own statement seemed to indicate that when he took the victim by the throat, he intended to kill her.

The only way that the case could be reduced to manslaughter was if the jury believed that there had been sufficient provocation. Could a quarrel between a man and a woman, during which she gave him a slap on the face, be regarded as sufficient provocation for him to kill her, asked the judge? In the history of human couples, such things must have happened very frequently.

It did not matter if the victim was killed by strangling with the hand or with the handkerchief, unless there was any real foundation for the story that the girl had the disease known as status lymphaticus, which Sir Bernard Spilsbury's evidence suggested was not the case. If the prisoner's subsequent account of killing the victim to prevent her from speaking to her uncle were to be believed, then the slap in the face he had supposedly received became irrelevant and his statement was not consistent with the assertion that he killed her in hot blood.

Finally, the judge asked if there was any room for belief even in the most sympathetic mind for the story of the boy's insanity. He had been given a good character by witnesses and nobody had noticed in him even the slightest signs of abnormality. Just because a man gave himself up for murder and didn't run away, it would be a dangerous precedent to suggest that gave evidence of insanity as required by the law.

The jury retired for twenty minutes before returning to the courtroom with their verdict. To the astonishment of everyone present, they found Boxall 'Not Guilty' on the charge of wilful murder against him but 'Guilty' of manslaughter.

'The jury have taken a merciful view of your case,' the judge told Boxall, sentencing him to twelve years' penal servitude.

22

'YOU HAVE GOT YOUR WORK TO DO'

Near Burford, 1931

At about half past eight on the night of 19 December 1931, two young men walking along the main Oxford to Cheltenham road came upon what looked like the scene of a road accident. Mrs Mabel Elizabeth Matthews had obviously fallen off her bicycle and was half sitting, half lying at the side of the road, bleeding heavily from her head and face, her bicycle on the ground nearby.

One of the men, farm labourer Frank Dumford, managed to flag down a passing car and the occupant, Mr Francis Fletcher, agreed to drive the injured woman to hospital. However, once inside the vehicle, Mrs Matthews struggled and fought so violently that Fletcher was unable to drive safely. Before long, he was forced to stop and, leaving Mrs Matthews with his wife on the side of the road, he continued into Burford, stopping at a hotel from where he called for a doctor.

Dr Walter Melville Forster was at the scene within minutes and found Mrs Matthews sitting on the kerb, moaning and moving her limbs convulsively and quite clearly near to death. Indeed, so severe were the injuries to her face and head that she died within ten minutes of his arrival.

Although Mrs Matthews's death at first seemed the result of a road accident, when police contacted her husband to break the news of the tragedy, it soon became evident that several items of her property were missing. The dead woman had left her home at about half past seven that evening, intending to cycle to Burford to do some shopping. When she set out, her bicycle had been fitted with an acetylene lamp and it now had no lamp at all, even though it would already have been dark when Mrs Matthews left home. Also missing were her purse and its

Burford, 1920s. (Author's collection)

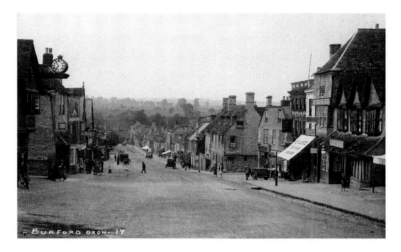

Burford. (Author's collection)

contents, the man's watch that she normally wore, a brown leather shopping bag containing the groceries she had purchased, a receipt for a year's subscription to a nursing association, a tin of 'Negroids' throat lozenges, an attaché case, brown suede gloves and a red celluloid cigarette case.

The police established that Mrs Matthews had reached Burford and purchased several items of groceries, including a jar of ginger, two tins of vegetable soup and a dough cake, which had been placed in a paper bag. She was last seen pushing her bicycle up the hill on the outskirts of the village, at which time she was smoking a cigarette. The police began a search for the missing items and were soon following a trail of Mrs Matthews's belongings along the main road.

Her spectacles and gloves were found near her bicycle. About a mile and a half further down the road towards Cheltenham, they found the jar of ginger, the

Negroids lozenges and an electric bicycle lamp, which bore no resemblance to the one that had been fitted to Mrs Matthews's bicycle. In the same location was a mackintosh coat, which did not belong to Mrs Matthews. In the pocket of the coat were a man's watch, similar to the one owned by Mrs Matthews, a gilt metal cigarette case and some sausage meat sandwiches.

Two miles further on, near the village of Windrush, Mrs Matthews's attaché case was found and 3 miles later, an empty paper bag identical to the one in which the dough cake had been placed. Roughly 10.5 miles from the scene of the 'accident' was the receipt for the subscription to the nursing association.

Sir Bernard Spilsbury was requested to carry out a post-mortem examination on the dead woman and discovered that Mrs Matthews had multiple injuries to her head, face and neck, including a fractured upper jaw. In addition, she had eleven broken ribs and extensive internal bruising, as well as the indisputable marks of an attempt at manual strangulation. Spilsbury concluded that, rather than being the victim of an accident, Mrs Matthews had been knocked off her bike and that someone had then knelt on her body and tried to strangle her, afterwards raining blows or kicks on her head and face. The cause of her death was given as shock and blood loss from her extensive injuries.

It seemed fairly obvious that whoever had abandoned the mackintosh, which appeared to be liberally stained with blood, had attacked Mrs Matthews. The fact that her cycle lamp had been stolen, and a different lamp was found with the mackintosh, suggested that the attacker had been another cyclist and indeed, a man had been seen pushing a bicycle without a light up the hill at Burford at about the same time that Mrs Matthews had been enjoying her last cigarette.

A message was circulated to all police forces advising them to be on the lookout for cyclists and, on 20 December, PC Morgan of the Monmouthshire Constabulary spoke to a man he saw pushing his bicycle near Abergavenny. The cyclist showed his military pass and told the policeman that he was George Thomas Pople, a private in the 2nd Battalion of the South Wales Borderers. He was currently on leave and was heading home to Brecon, having spent the last few days visiting relatives in Bournemouth and Northolt. He had cycled homewards through Bath, Gloucester and Ross and, when told that Morgan was making enquiries about the death of a female cyclist at Burford, near Oxford, he seemed quite unperturbed. 'You have got your work to do,' he said equably then denied having been anywhere near the area. Pople was later to call at the Brecon police station for some carbide for his bicycle lamp, where it was noted that he kept his gloves on all the while.

On the following day, Sergeant John Mitchell, a Brecon police officer, called at Pople's home to question him further about his movements. Pople gave a statement but his answers seemed vague to Mitchell and he noticed that Pople's hands were covered in fresh scratches and abrasions. Detective Inspector E.J. Rippington was hastily summoned from Oxford to Brecon and, having questioned Pople at the police station there, he produced the mackintosh and asked Pople if it belonged to him. 'Yes,' replied Pople.

Asked by Rippington to account for his whereabouts on 19 December, Pople refused, telling Rippington that he had said all he was going to say. Unfortunately, when he had given his statement to Sergeant Mitchell, Pople had not been under caution. Nevertheless, Rippington informed him that he would be taken to Burford and charged with the murder of Mrs Matthews. 'I said all I had to say last night,' responded Pople.

Pople and his bicycle were transported to Burford police station by car and formally charged. A magistrate, Mr H.G. Piggott, had been summoned to the police station and remanded Pople for eight days to allow the police to complete their enquiries.

By the time twenty-two-year-old Private Pople appeared at a hearing before magistrates in mid January 1932, the police had sent several items of evidence to Home Office Analyst Dr Roche Lynch. Pople had admitted owning the mackintosh and human blood had been found on the right sleeve. Blood had also been found on the right-hand sleeve of Pople's jacket and on the right-hand cuff of his shirt, the pattern of the bloodstains on the three garments were consistent with them all having been worn on top of each other. Roche Lynch also found blood on the tie that Pople had been wearing, on one of his shoes and on the electric bicycle lamp, although in insufficient quantities to determine whether the blood was human or animal in origin.

Pople's home had been searched on Christmas Day 1931 and an acetylene lamp, similar to that owned by Mrs Matthews, was found in a sealed box in a garden shed.

Committed for trial by magistrates at Burford for the murder of Mrs Matthews, Pople appeared before Mr Justice Roche at the Gloucester Assizes, which opened on 1 February 1932. The case was prosecuted by Sir Reginald Coventry KC and Mr G.K. Rose, while Dr W.G. Earengey and Mr E.R. Guest acted for the defence.

Pople, who pleaded 'Not Guilty', had now admitted being involved in the death of Mrs Matthews, although he maintained that her death had been more the result of a tragic accident than of murder. According to Pople, he had been staying with his wife and mother-in-law at Brecon, on a month's leave from his regiment, which had begun on 9 December 1931.

He had decided to visit relatives and had cycled to Bath and then on to London, leaving the capital on 19 December, intending to return to Brecon. Joseph Maddams, with whom he had been staying, provided him with some sausage sandwiches for the journey. As darkness fell, he realised that his lamp had stopped working and, as he pushed his bicycle along the lane near Burford, he had seen the lights of another cycle heading towards him and, having no money, decided to steal the cyclist's lamp.

As the cycle drew level with him in the dark, he reached out to snatch the lamp but overbalanced as he did so, falling into the bicycle and unseating its rider, who fell off her machine and struck a telegraph pole. Pople admitted that he had picked up some of Mrs Matthews's belongings, which were scattered over the road.

However, in accounting for Mrs Matthews's death, Pople had reckoned without the persistence of Sir Bernard Spilsbury, who categorically denied that her injuries could possibly have occurred in the way he described. Illustrating his arguments with a wax model of a human head and neck, similar to those used to display hats in milliner's shops, Spilsbury insisted that blows or kicks were the only possible explanation for all of the dead woman's injuries, with the exception of the attempt at strangulation.

Defence counsel Dr Earengey tried a number of different alternative explanations. Had Spilsbury considered the possibility of a person coming into contact with a telegraph pole, then striking a second post or wire strut and afterwards coming into contact with large pieces of rough Cotswold stone, before ending up against a wall made from the same rough stone? Spilsbury assured the court that he had considered and dismissed just such a scenario.

'Are the injuries to the face entirely consistent with the suggestion I am putting forward?' asked Earengey.

'I do not think they are,' argued Spilsbury.

'Will you swear that the injuries on the back of the head could not have been caused by falling against the sharp surface of a piece of Cotswold stone?' Earengey persisted.

Spilsbury continued to insist that the injuries had been caused by violent, glancing blows, such as those from punches or kicks and, when Sir Reginald Coventry produced the pair of black shoes with pointed toes owned by Pople, Spilsbury agreed that Mrs Matthews's head wounds were consistent with kicks from a person wearing them.

Sergeant Jones from Burford, who had investigated the 'accident', told the court that he had not noticed any large pieces of Cotswold stone on the grass verge. Since the presence of this stone was crucial to the defence, it was agreed that someone would be despatched to the site to check.

Meanwhile, Mr Justice Roche asked Spilsbury: if a body was thrown violently against a telegraph pole and any part of that body was bleeding, would he expect to find marks of blood on that pole?

'Yes, certainly,' replied Spilsbury.

'And if the body came in contact with a stone, causing bleeding, what would you find then?' asked the judge.

'There would certainly be some blood on the stone,' asserted Spilsbury.

Spilsbury's refusal to be budged on his conclusions effectively brought about the collapse of the entire case for the defence, particularly when it was established that the grass verge had been re-examined and no pieces of stone had been found there.

There was, of course, other evidence against the defendant but, other than the bloodstains on his clothing, it was largely circumstantial. A lamp, similar to that owned by Mrs Matthews had been found in his garden shed, although it was impossible to prove that it was the actual lamp stolen from the dead woman's bicycle.

The bloodstained mackintosh was positively identified by Pople's mother-in-law, Mrs Jane Morris, as one that she had given to him before he set out on his trip. She told the court that, on his return, Pople had said that he had thrown the coat away because the sleeves were too short. The mackintosh was produced in court and the prosecution pointed out two buttons on it that didn't match the rest, which Mrs Morris said that she had sewn on hurriedly with white cotton.

Pople had been identified by two witnesses who had attended an identity parade after his arrest. Miss Isabella Hurdman owned a café in Cheltenham and stated that Pople had arrived at her premises between 9.30 and 10 p.m. on the night of 19 December and had stayed the night there, paying four shillings for bed and breakfast. This negated Pople's explanation that he had stolen the cycle lamp because he had no money to replace his own defective one.

Joiner Frederick Harrington had met Pople cycling at Dashwood Hill, West Wycombe at 2.15 p.m. on the afternoon of 19 December. The two had cycled together for more than an hour, with Pople telling Harrington that he had come from Northolt and was heading for Brecon. Harrington recalled a mackintosh coat being draped over the crossbar of Pople's bicycle, yet, according to Miss Hurdman, when Pople arrived at her café, he did not have an overcoat with him. With witnesses able to place Pople at Cheltenham and West Wycombe at specific times, it was possible to calculate his progress between the two points, which put him near Burford at around the time of the attack on Mrs Matthews.

Yet the most compelling evidence for the jury was that of the unshakeable Sir Bernard Spilsbury and, in the face of it, Pople's defence collapsed completely. The jury were quick to find him 'Guilty' of the wilful murder of Mrs Matthews, having completely dismissed his rather far-fetched story, which seemed to suggest that after accidentally falling from her bicycle, Mrs Matthews had somehow collided with several objects before finally coming to rest on the grass verge.

Pople stood to attention in the dock, tears streaming silently down his cheeks as Mr Justice Roche pronounced the death sentence. His defence counsel immediately announced that they intended to appeal his conviction.

The appeal was heard at the Court of Criminal Appeal before Lord Hewart, the Chief Justice, along with Mr Justice MacKinnon and Mr Justice Hawke. Mr Guest, speaking on behalf of the defendant, admitted that there had been a case to answer and that he could find nothing to criticise about the summary of the case made by Mr Justice Roche. However, he believed that the proper verdict was one of manslaughter rather than murder and maintained that, on the evidence heard in court, no reasonable body of men could have come to the conclusion to which the jury came.

The court of appeal ruled that Mr Justice Roche had summarised the evidence most fairly and that he had quite clearly instructed the jury that if they accepted Pople's version of the events of 19 December 1931 then a verdict of manslaughter would be justified. Yet the jury were quite entitled to return a verdict of murder and the appeal court saw no reason to challenge this decision.

His appeal having failed, George Thomas Pople was executed at Oxford on 1 April 1932.

23

'SOONER OR LATER THE REAL TRUTH WILL BE REVEALED TO YOU ALL'

Oxford, 1931

Fifty-eight-year-old widow Annie Louisa Kempson had made plans to go and stay with Mrs Annie Smith, a friend in West Hampstead, London. When she didn't arrive as arranged on Sunday, 2 August 1931, Mrs Smith contacted Mrs Kempson's brother to ask him to check on his sister. George Reynolds, who worked as a college servant at Jesus College, went to his sister's house in St Clements but, when his knocks at the door elicited no response, he initially assumed that Annie had taken a later bus than expected and was *en route* to London. When her friend reported that there was still no sign of her, Reynolds went back to the house with his son, Albert, on the evening of Monday 3 August. Albert managed to gain entry through an upstairs window, letting his father in through the front door. The two men found Mrs Kempson's body lying on the floor, covered with rugs and cushions, in one of the rooms at the back of the house.

The police were called and almost immediately requested the assistance of Scotland Yard, which came in the person of Detective Chief Inspector 'Lucky John' Horwell, who was accompanied by Detective Sergeant Rees. Horwell's first action was to request a post-mortem examination, which was carried out by police surgeon Dr Francis H. Dixon, with a subsequent three-hour examination by Sir Bernard Spilsbury. The preliminary findings indicated that Annie Kempson had received

St Clements Street,
Oxford. (© N. Sly)

St Clements Street.
(© N. Sly)

at least three blows to the head with a blunt instrument such as a hammer before being stabbed in the throat with something resembling a chisel, severing her carotid artery and causing her to bleed to death. There was nothing to suggest that Annie Kempson had struggled or tried to defend herself against her killer and no signs of forced entry into the house. She had most probably been stunned by an initial blow to the back of the head and had her other injuries inflicted after she had fallen to the ground. The presence of blood in her lungs meant that she had not died instantly but had continued breathing for some time after the weapon was plunged through her throat from ear to ear.

The doctors found it impossible to reliably estimate a time of death, although Spilsbury was able to say that Mrs Kempson had died within twelve hours of eating a meal of tomatoes and within one or two hours of eating some bread and butter and possibly some custard. Mrs Kempson's wristwatch had stopped at 2.27. None of her clothing had been disturbed and although her home had been ransacked and there appeared to be some money missing, £30 had been left untouched in the house.

In the year prior to Mrs Kempson's death, her house had been burgled several times and the burglaries reported to the police. According to a near neighbour, the purpose of the burglaries seemed to have been more to annoy or frighten Mrs Kempson than to steal anything of any value. The police were quick to point out that the previous thefts were petty in comparison to the last attack on Mrs Kempson, whose wounds had been inflicted with such force that the police believed that they were the work of a maniac.

From what was known of Mrs Kempson's regular habits, her death was estimated to have occurred shortly after breakfast on the morning of Saturday 1 August. On the previous day, she had spent some time with a friend, Mrs Steele, who had left her alive and well at seven o'clock in the evening. Mrs Kempson had bought some new shoes on 31 July and Mrs Steele had carried them for her, eventually taking the shoes home with her. When she tried to drop them off at Mrs Kempson's at eleven o'clock the next morning, there was no response to her knocks or ringing of the doorbell and she eventually put them through an open window, where they were later found by police searching the house after the discovery of Mrs Kempson's body. Mrs Kempson normally visited her husband's grave every Saturday afternoon to lay fresh flowers and clean the headstone but had made no such visit on 1 August. When her body was found, she was still wearing her hair curlers, which she was known to remove shortly after breakfast every day.

The police began their enquiries in the neighbourhood of Boundary House, Mrs Kempson's home, and soon established that a number of strangers had been seen in the area at around the time of her death. Initially of most interest was a ginger-haired man, aged around forty, who was believed to have been selling *Old Moore's Almanac* door-to-door. (According to the newspapers of the time, the almanac for 1931 forecast a general increase in crime, particularly in sensational murder cases, one of which would be the brutal murder of a woman at Oxford.)

Within ten days of the murder, more than 3,000 people had been interviewed, including the almanac seller who, having satisfactorily accounted for his movements, was quickly eliminated from the investigation. However, that still left a surprisingly large number of strangers unaccounted for, including a man described as an insurance man or salesman who had been working in the area and was seen to call at Boundary House on the afternoon of Saturday 1 August. There was also a scruffily dressed man with a ruddy complexion and a gruff voice, a man who had threatened a dog and its owner with a knife, a 'snarling man', and a man who had knocked on the door of a nearby house earlier in the week and demanded three shillings from the daughter of the owner, saying that he had delivered a garden seat and some roofing felt. Finally, a caller had been seen being admitted to Boundary House by Mrs Kempson on the morning of 1 August. He was described as being between thirty-five and forty years old, of medium build, thick set and around 5ft 4in tall, with dark hair. He was wearing a dark coloured jacket with either fawn or dark trousers and carried a mackintosh slung over his left shoulder. Two witnesses independently described what police believed was the same man. The first, housemaid Violet Reeves, who worked at the Duke of Edinburgh public house, located almost opposite Boundary House, had seen him knocking on Mrs Kempson's door at between 9.40 and 9.50 on the morning of 1 August. The second witness, a house painter named George Horne, was even more precise with his timing, telling police that he had seen Mrs Kempson letting the man into the house at 9.56 a.m. As Mrs Kempson was thought to have been killed shortly after breakfast, both of these sightings came at what was considered to be a crucial time.

As well as trying to trace everyone who had been in the area at the time, legitimately or otherwise, the police also conducted a fingertip search for the murder weapon or weapons. Following a tip from an Oxford street seller, who reported two men spending money very freely at a hotel in Cowley, one of whom bore a strong resemblance to the 'snarling man', the search was extended to allotments and gardens in that area too. Boundary House was very close to the River Cherwell and the police used punts to drag the water. Mrs Kempson was known to have recently made a new will and the police appealed for the person who had sold her the do-it-yourself will form, found in a locked cupboard in the house after her death, to come forward. They were hampered in their search of the property by Mrs Kempson's reluctance to throw anything away, which had led to her house becoming cluttered with boxes and boxes of 'useful' items. It became a major task for the police to sort through the detritus of her life, cataloguing every item and seeking anything that might shed some light on her death.

On 13 August, the police issued a statement to the press saying that they had received a large number of anonymous letters about the murder, some of which contained what they described as 'very interesting and helpful information'. They appealed to the writers of these letters to come forward, stressing that any assistance given would be treated in the strictest confidence.

However, the first real lead came from a Mrs Alice Andrews, a widow who lived in Gypsy Lane, Oxford. In 1929 Mrs Andrews had bought a vacuum cleaner from a door-to-door salesman named Henry Daniel Seymour. She had continued to buy various goods from

The Duke public house (formerly the Duke of Edinburgh). (© N. Sly)

Seymour and, on 31 July 1931, had bumped into him in the street and stopped for a chat.

Seymour had told her that he was planning to go for a swim in the river at Eynsham but was undecided since the weather was quite dull. At eight o'clock that evening, Seymour knocked on the door of her house. He told Mrs Andrews that while he had been swimming he had noticed some boys rifling through the pockets of his coat, which he had left on the bank. When he had got out of the water to try and stop them, the boys had run off, taking with them his wallet, containing thirty shillings. Seymour asked if Mrs Andrews could possibly lend him a little money, as he wanted to go to Thame and had no money for the bus fare. Mrs Andrews gave him four shillings and sixpence and he promised to return it immediately after the weekend. However, just two hours later, Seymour was back. When Mrs Andrews's son answered the door, Seymour asked if he could speak to his mother, telling Mrs Andrews that he had missed the last bus and asking if she could give him a bed for the night.

Seymour left two small parcels on the hall table overnight, which Mrs Andrews noticed contained a hammer and a chisel. When he left her house at ten minutes to ten on 1 August, the hammer and chisel were in the pocket of the raincoat he wore over his dark, double-breasted suit. Seymour was next seen between eleven o'clock and half past eleven at a bus stop in London Road, Headington, when he was described as being 'agitated'. He told Mrs Florence Collins, also a previous customer, that he was heading to Brighton for a holiday, explaining his agitation by saying that he had just been involved in a car accident. Seymour was positively identified as a passenger on the 11.03 a.m. bus to Aylesbury and, later that afternoon, was at the Greyhound Hotel in the town. He had recently stayed at the hotel, leaving without paying his bill. Once again, he was described as 'upset' by hoteliers Mr and Mrs Parkinson, but they put this down to the fact that he had tried to sneak into the hotel without being observed and had been discovered in his room, searching through the two suitcases he had left there on the pretext of wanting to retrieve his shaving kit. Mr Parkinson told Seymour that the police had been contacted and asked him to settle his outstanding bill, which Seymour promised to do as soon as he had been for some food. Not surprisingly, he didn't return.

The police were immediately interested in Henry Seymour's movements, since his business card had been one of several found behind a clock on the mantelpiece at Mrs Kempson's home. He was apprehended at his flat in Brighton and Horwell and Rees immediately went to question him, carrying with them a warrant for his arrest on a charge of embezzlement of funds from his current employers. They interviewed Seymour at Brighton police station and, after asking the officers to identify themselves, he asked them why they wanted to question him. 'Is it about this murder in Oxford?' Seymour asked and, when told that it was, he continued, 'My head has been so dizzy these last few weeks and what with my motor accident and my bad nerves, I shall have to think very slowly and that will give you time to write every word I want.'

Seymour then gave an account of his movements around the time of the murder, categorically denying that he had either seen Mrs Kempson or knocked on her door during the time he was in Oxford. He told Horwell that he had read about the murder in the newspapers and, beyond what he had read, emphatically denied having any knowledge of the murder whatsoever. 'I have a lot of trouble but I don't kill people,' stated Seymour. By now, the investigating officers were aware that Seymour was wanted by their colleagues in the Devon and Cornwall Constabulary, having been bound over and fined for causing grievous bodily harm to a Paignton woman, whom he had attacked in her own home after trying to sell her a vacuum cleaner. Ordered by the court to pay £10 compensation to his victim, Seymour had absconded without paying. Not only that but he also had a string of previous convictions for house-breaking, robbery and burglary dating back to 1906 and had served time in prison.

Meanwhile, the police had recovered his suitcases from the Greyhound Hotel and, while they found no chisels or similar implements, the cases did contain a brand new hammer, a steel case opener and a new brace and 1-inch bit. Where the shaft joined the head of the hammer, there were some small threads of cloth and, although there were no traces of blood found on the hammer, it had obviously been recently washed.

In spite of his denials, Seymour was arrested and charged with Mrs Kempson's murder, eventually standing trial before Mr Justice Swift at the Oxford Assizes. Mr St John G. Micklethwait KC and Mr Wilfrid Price prosecuted the case, while Seymour was granted legal aid to engage Dr W.G. Earengey KC and Mr E.R. Guest to handle his defence.

The case for the prosecution was straightforward. They maintained that Seymour had been admitted to Boundary House by Mrs Kempson and had then proceeded to ransack the house in search of money. Mrs Andrews testified that Seymour had a hammer and chisel in his possession on the morning of the murder, although the defence countered by reminding the court that he had openly left them in plain view on her hall table overnight and made no attempt to conceal them from her. Mr Albert Fulkes told the court that he had sold a new hammer to a man resembling Seymour on 31 July, although the defence made much of the fact that Fulkes was unable to positively identify Seymour as his customer, nor did any record of the sale appear on the shop's till roll for that day.

Mrs Isobel Bellmore, who was Seymour's landlady in Brighton and knew him as 'Mr Harvey', told the court that her lodger had been away for a few days, arriving home at 8 p.m. on 1 August. She too described Seymour as being 'agitated' on his return but said that he had told her that his wife had left him and that his luggage had been stolen on the train journey to Brighton. When the police searched Seymour's room in Brighton, they discovered that holes had been made in the floorboards, giving the occupant a view of Mrs Bellmore's bedroom below. Whether this had been done for voyeuristic purposes or to try and discover where Mrs Bellmore kept her money was debatable although, in the strict moral climate of the day, the revelation that Seymour had recently walked out on his wife and ten-year-old son did little to endear him to the jury.

The medical witnesses stated that, although it had proved impossible to pinpoint the exact time of Mrs Kempson's death from the condition of her body, their knowledge of her regular habits made it most likely that she had been killed between eight o'clock and midday on 1 August. Seymour had left Mrs Andrews's home at about ten minutes to ten and had caught a bus at three minutes past eleven, leaving him roughly an hour in which to commit the murder. However, the defence insisted that it was not possible for him to get from Mrs Andrews's home to the bus stop and still have time to kill Mrs Kempson and ransack her house. They then proceeded to call a number of witnesses who were all absolutely positive that they had seen Mrs Kempson alive and well much later in the day.

A bricklayer named William Low stated that he had known Mrs Kempson well and was sure that he had seen her walking from the direction of her home at twenty past eleven on the morning of 1 August. Low said that Mrs Kempson had stopped at a postbox, then crossed the road and continued to walk away from her home towards the shops. Cross-examined by Mr Micklethwait, who suggested that Low had actually seen Mrs Kempson on 30 July, when she was known to have posted a card to her friend, Low insisted that 30 July would have been a Thursday and he would have been at work. He had made a point of contacting the police soon after the murder was discovered to tell them what he knew.

Evelyn Barrett, an assistant at a baker's shop in Oxford, remembered serving Mrs Kempson late on the morning of 1 August. She particularly recalled it being a Saturday and that Mrs Kempson had told her that she was planning to go away to London the next day. Mrs Sarah King, who had also known Mrs Kempson well, had already independently corroborated Evelyn Barrett's evidence, having told the police that she had seen Mrs Kempson entering the baker's at about half past eleven, when Mrs Kempson had nodded and smiled at her.

A grocer's assistant had served Mrs Kempson at between midday and one o'clock on 1 August. His employer, George Woodward, agreed, also adding that he had seen Mrs Kempson at the shop on the evening of 31 July and that, when he had left work at half past nine that evening, there had been a man hanging about outside. Woodward described the loitering man as just over 5ft tall, stockily built and wearing a rather dirty blue suit with a collarless shirt. The man's appearance had caused Woodward some concern in view of the money left at his shop overnight.

Frederick Taylor, a master painter, had known Mrs Kempson for more than twenty years and had seen her at around half past twelve in the afternoon, while Mrs Kate Barson, who had known Mrs Kempson all her life, had seen her near her home at between 2.50 p.m. and 3 p.m. Her husband, who also knew Mrs Kempson well, corroborated his wife's account, saying that they were so close to Mrs Kempson that she would actually have bumped into him had his wife not grabbed his arm and pulled him out of the way. Finally, Mrs Florence Kirk had seen Mrs Kempson on Cornmarket Street on the evening of 1 August at between

*Cornmarket Street,
where Florence
Kirk spotted
Mrs Kempson.
(Author's
collection)*

five o'clock and half past five. The prosecution's response to the various sightings was to insist that all the witnesses had been mistaken about the date.

Seymour then went into the witness box to speak in his own defence. He stated that he had worked for the Tellus Vacuum Cleaner Company as a door-to-door salesman. He had called on Mrs Kempson in around June 1929 and left his card with her then. He had since left Tellus and was now working as a salesman for a firm called Yarnstrong Ltd, although he admitted that, since starting work with his new company, he had called on some of the customers to whom he had previously sold Tellus products.

Seymour admitted that he had got himself into accounting difficulties with Yarnstrong Ltd by collecting money for goods sold and not passing it on to the company. In May or June of 1931, he had been asked to clear up certain misappropriations of company funds and, knowing that he was likely to be arrested, had left his wife and child in Oxford and fled to Brighton, believing that he would be able to get another job and earn sufficient money to clear his outstanding debts.

On a return visit to Oxford, he had approached his former address and seen a man standing outside his house. Believing the man to be a detective, he had not stopped but had driven on and later had a car accident, which had rendered him unconscious. Having woken up on the side of the road, he had contacted the owner of the hired car then driven on to Folkestone and later Aylesbury, where he planned to collect some accounts.

He had visited Oxford again on 31 July and bought a bathing costume, a towel and some tools. He had decided to look for a woodworking job and told the court that he intended to pick up a few tools here and there so as to avoid a large expenditure at one time. His intention had been to visit his wife and son but it occurred to him that the police might well have his old home under surveillance. So he had gone to bathe in the river at Pink Hill, where his wallet had been stolen, leaving him with around fifteen or sixteen shillings in loose change in his trouser pocket.

Having visited a roadside café for tea and biscuits, he called on Mrs Andrews to borrow money then went back to her house to ask for accommodation, having missed the last bus. After leaving Mrs Andrews's home in the morning, he had walked to Wheatley and caught a bus to Aylesbury, where he placed his new tools in his suitcase at the hotel. He then caught a bus to London and travelled on to Brighton by train.

Seymour admitted giving his landlady in Brighton a false name, saying that he was afraid that the police were looking for him for misappropriation of funds from his employer. He had also given a false name to the other driver involved in the car accident.

A representative from Yarnstrong Ltd, Mr Oscar Neville, told the court that Seymour owed the firm £96. He also owed £25 to the proprietor of a garage in Oxford who had towed his accident-damaged car.

Under cross-examination, Seymour denied knowing anything at all about Mrs Kempson's financial circumstances. Indeed, it was widely assumed in the area that Mrs Kempson was wealthier than she actually was, since the majority of her money was tied up in property. Seymour vehemently denied buying the tools with the intention of either robbing or killing Mrs Kempson or anyone else for that matter. He admitted that he was short of money but insisted that he had fully intended to get a new job and pay off his debts in full. He also denied abandoning his wife and child, saying that he had desperately wanted to see them, but was too afraid that his old home was being watched by the police.

The final witnesses for the defence were able to identify Seymour as having visited the tearooms on 31 July and it was then left to the opposing counsels and the judge to sum up the case for the jury.

Dr Earengey, for the defence, argued that Mrs Kempson's death had occurred not on Saturday morning on 1 August but either that evening or even on the following morning, when the defendant had been nowhere near the area. He reminded the jury of the number of witnesses who had testified to seeing the deceased alive and well much later in the day at a time when, if the prosecution were to be believed, she had already been dead for several hours. Most of those witnesses had known Mrs Kempson for many years and yet the prosecution could offer no explanation for their evidence other than that they had all been mistaken about the date. True, Mrs Kempson had been found wearing her curlers but, if she habitually took them out after breakfast every morning then she must also have habitually put them in every night before retiring to bed and would surely have taken them out on Sunday morning as well as on Saturday, had she been alive.

The defence then dealt with the supposed murder weapons. They reminded the jury that no chisel, screwdriver or similar tool had ever been found in Seymour's possession, neither was there any record of him ever buying such items. Even if, as Mrs Andrews had testified, he had been in possession of a chisel on the morning of the murder, he had left it in plain view with the hammer on her hall table overnight, as he had later left the hammer in an open suitcase at the Greyhound Hotel. Would a murderer leave the murder weapon – the very evidence of his guilt – in a suitcase in a hotel room where the police would be sure to find it?

Dr Earengey then addressed Mrs Kempson's injuries. Sir Bernard Spilsbury had already said in court that the head of the hammer found in Seymour's suitcase was too small to have inflicted Mrs Kempson's head wounds and of course no traces of blood or hair had ever been found on it. The prosecution argued that the hammer head had been wrapped in a piece of cloth, accounting for the threads found between the head and the handle but, even if this were the case, then there was no blood found on the threads either.

The prosecution insisted that there was no question about the time of Mrs Kempson's death and that Seymour's conduct throughout was indicative of his guilt. He had been desperately in need of money and had gone to Mrs Kempson's home, knowing full well that she often kept large sums of money there since she had once purchased something from him and paid for her purchase with £5 notes. He had bought his tools expressly to burgle Mrs Kempson and, because she knew him and would be able to identify him to the police, had no alternative but to kill her when he found her at home.

He had invented stories about a nervous condition, his wife leaving him and his luggage being stolen to cover his agitation at having committed the murder of an elderly lady described by all who knew her as 'a dear little inoffensive woman'. The prosecution did not deny that Seymour had been involved in a car accident that might well have upset him but reminded the jury that the accident had actually occurred on 22 June and that nobody had seen any signs of nerves or agitation whatsoever in Seymour prior to 1 August.

Mr Justice Swift urged the jury to ignore anything they might have read about the case in the newspapers and concentrate on the facts they had heard in court. It had been clearly established that, apart from a brief window of time, Seymour had no opportunity to commit the murder. Thus establishing the time of Mrs Kempson's death was the crux of the case and Sir Bernard Spilsbury had stressed that he was unable to narrow that time down within twenty-four or thirty-six hours, although Dr Dixon had been slightly more confident that death had occurred on the Saturday morning.

Both pathologists agreed that Mrs Kempson had eaten a meal of tomatoes around twelve hours before her death. If she had died on Saturday evening, or even Sunday morning, where were the remains of those tomatoes and the bread and butter she had supposedly eaten shortly before her death? The police had found the table still set with the breakfast dishes left over from the meal eaten by Mrs Kempson's lodger, Miss Eleanor Jane Williams. The table was exactly as it was when Miss Williams left the house for a short holiday with friends at 9.20 a.m. on 1 August and had not been cleared. Furthermore, Mrs Kempson was wearing overalls and her curlers when she was found, which suggested that she had not left home that morning.

Finally, Mr Justice Swift asked the jury to consider the identity of the man seen being admitted by Mrs Kempson to her house at around 10.30 a.m. on 1 August.

Who was this man and, if he was on legitimate business, why had he not come forward in response to police appeals?

The jury retired for about three quarters of an hour before returning to pronounce Seymour 'Guilty'. Mr Swift turned to the defendant and asked if he had anything to say why judgement of death should not be passed on him. 'Only this,' said Seymour, continuing:

> I am convinced that sooner or later the real truth will be revealed to you all. When that time comes you will remember my last words. Before God and my fellow man I swear that I did not kill or hurt Mrs Kempson and, further, that I cannot conceive of any question of difficulty financially or any temptation of money or anything else that would have tempted me to commit this fiendish murder. I could not have done it. I cannot say any more.

As soon as the death sentence was passed on Seymour his counsel immediately announced their intention to appeal his conviction and the appeal was heard in November 1931 before the Lord Chief Justice, Mr Justice Avory and Mr Justice Hawke.

Once again, the defence argued the timing of the murder, saying that if Mrs Kempson was alive much after 10.30 a.m. on the morning of 1 August, then Seymour could not possibly have killed her. He had caught a bus at 11.03 a.m. at a bus stop that was twenty-two minutes walk away from Boundary House.

In his original summary for the jury, Mr Justice Swift had pointed out that the table still bearing the remnants of a meal eaten by Mrs Kempson's lodger and the fact that the bed was unmade were evidence that the old lady had died on Saturday morning. This was not conclusive evidence, as there was nothing to suggest that Mrs Kempson would definitely have cleared the table but could just as easily have left it exactly as it was without bothering to clear it or make her bed.

The defence counsel argued that Mr Justice Swift had placed too much emphasis on the evidence of surgeon Dr Dixon and too little on that of Sir Bernard Spilsbury, whose evidence he had brushed aside. At very least, he should have made more of their differences of opinion to the jury. Swift had also told the jury that most of the witnesses in the case had spoken to the press and what he described as their 'so-called evidence' had appeared in the newspapers before the police had been made aware of it. Dr Earengey told the appeal court that the great majority of the witnesses had denied being interviewed by the press at all and that all had given official statements to the police before any of their remarks had been quoted.

Finally, the defence told the court of appeal that Mr Justice Swift had informed the jury that Seymour had admitted to having a screwdriver in his possession, even though the pathologists had clearly stated that a screwdriver could not have made the wound in Mrs Kempson's neck.

Mr Micklethwait, for the prosecution, reminded the appeal court that the wounds on Mrs Kempson's head had not killed her immediately and there was a possibility that Seymour had ransacked the house while the victim lay unconscious and dying, rather than having first killed her and then ransacked the house. This would have allowed him sufficient time to attack Mrs Kempson and still be at the bus stop to catch the 11.03 a.m. bus.

It was Mrs Kempson's normal routine to visit her husband's grave every Saturday afternoon and the fact that she had not done this on 1 August was consistent with her having been attacked and killed that morning. Moreover, the judge had repeatedly reminded the jury that, if they had any doubts whatsoever then they should give the defendant the benefit of those doubts.

The Lord Chief Justice stated that the appeal raised two main questions. One was the time of Mrs Kempson's death and the second was whether or not Seymour actually murdered her.

On the first question, they believed that the prosecution had shown beyond reasonable doubt that Mrs Kempson had died on Saturday morning. She had not visited her husband's grave and, although she had expected her shoes to be delivered that morning, had not answered the door. The fact that she was going on holiday the next day could be seen as an added incentive for her to ensure her house was clean and tidy, making it unlikely that she would have neglected to make her bed or clear the breakfast table. It also placed doubt on the dates of some of the witness sightings of Mrs Kempson later in the day, since she would have little need of groceries, knowing that she would be away from home. Thus there seemed to be ample evidence that Mrs Kempson died on the morning of 1 August.

Seymour's movements seemed to be motivated by a desire to avoid being arrested for embezzling money from his employers. If this was the case, why did he stay in Oxford overnight on 31 July rather than returning to his hotel in Aylesbury? Why did he not return to Aylesbury earlier on the morning of 1 August? And, if he was so short of money, why had he not collected more of the payments owed him by people in the area?

Dismissing Mr Justice Swift's remarks about witnesses speaking to the press as 'a slip', the appeal judges determined that his summary had, as a whole, been fair and adequate. Therefore, after giving the appeal their careful consideration, they had come to the conclusion that it had failed.

Thus ended thirty-nine-year-old Henry Daniel Seymour's last chance for a reprieve of his death sentence and he went to the gallows at Oxford Prison on 10 December 1931, protesting his innocence to the end.

Note: In some accounts of the case in the contemporary newspapers, Mrs Kempson's name is given as Alice rather than Annie. Witness Mr Low is also called Mr Law and Kate Barson is alternatively named Kate Baron or Barron. Violet Reeves is also referred to as Violet Reeds, witness Mr Horne's first name is given as either James or George and Mrs Steele is frequently named Miss Steel. Detective Sergeant Rees's name is alternatively spelled Reece.

24

'THERE WAS GOING TO BE A ROW AND I WALKED AWAY'

Shutford, 1935

August 1935 saw seemingly endless days of blue skies and sunshine – a heatwave that had already lasted for two weeks and showed no sign of ending. The extreme heat had caused many frayed tempers since it began, with people looking forward to the day when the weather finally broke and the scorched countryside was cooled by rain. However, the organisers of the village fête in Shutford were doubtless crossing their fingers that Saturday 10 August 1935 would remain rain free.

Fortunately, the day was fine and everyone seemed to enjoy the fête, which featured several sporting competitions along with the usual games, sideshows and stalls and ended with dancing. Brothers Joseph and William Messenger cycled to the fête from the neighbouring village of Epwell and had such a good time that they stayed much later than they had intended. When the time came for them to leave, both realised that they had no lamps on their bicycles and made a decision to leave their cycles with a friend and take the bus home. It was a decision that was to cost them both dearly.

The Messenger brothers climbed aboard the bus driven by Archibald Handcock when it stopped outside the forge in Shutford village at just before midnight. At the same time, Mrs Hilda May Gibbs, who lived at the forge, and her sister, Miss Ivy Cora Goode, were about to alight from the bus, when there was a sudden loud bang. 'I've got a tyre burst,' said the bus driver, Mr Handcock, but, no sooner had the words left his mouth, than there was a second retort and it became obvious that the noises had nothing whatsoever to do with bus tyres but were in fact gun shots.

Twenty-four-year-old Mrs Gibbs was standing by the door about to step off the bus when a bullet hit her squarely in the chest. 'My husband's shot me,' she said in apparent surprise before falling to the floor of the bus. The bullet passed straight through Mrs Gibbs's chest and on through the bus window, finally going through the window of a cottage opposite. The second bullet passed right through Ivy Goode's groin before hitting Joseph Messenger, travelling through both of his legs and then shattering the kneecap of his brother, William, remaining lodged in his leg. 'I've got it as well,' said Joseph Messenger but, by that time, everyone's attention was focused on helping the two injured women and nobody realised that he was gradually bleeding to death. The sound of a third shot, which appeared to come from a stone barn at the side of the road, went almost unnoticed in the chaos.

The Shutford village policeman, PC Rand, was quickly on the scene and ordered Archibald Handcock to drive his bus straight to the hospital at Banbury. There had been nine passengers on the bus as well as the driver and Ernest Kempton, the conductor, and all those passengers who were uninjured remained on board to render what first aid they could to those wounded. As the bus hurtled along the country lanes at breakneck speed, Joseph Messenger coughed repeatedly, while Ivy Goode, who was still conscious, asked over and over again, 'Am I going to die?' PC Norman Benham was sent to the hospital to interview the survivors, while PC Rand began a search of the immediate area. When he was informed by a witness that a third shot had been heard, Rand checked the barn, where he found the body of a young man, with a service rifle laying on the ground beside him. The breech of the gun held a cartridge case and a second lay on the cowshed floor – a third was discovered close by in the light of the following day.

The dead man was quickly identified as twenty-five-year-old village blacksmith Wilfred Gibbs, the estranged husband of Hilda, who had taken the first bullet as she prepared to leave the bus. Photographs of Hilda and the couple's baby were found in Wilfred's breast pocket.

In the early hours of Sunday morning, PC Benham was at the Horton Hospital, Banbury, taking a deposition from Mrs Gibbs who was still conscious, although obviously dying from the wound in her chest. He asked her, 'How did you receive your injuries?'

'I was shot.'

'Who did it?'

'My husband, I expect.'

'Did you see him?'

'No.'

'Has he threatened to take your life?'

'Yes.'

Hilda Gibbs died soon after giving her statement to PC Benham, while her twenty-one-year-old sister died just before 3 a.m. and Joseph Messenger had already been pronounced dead shortly after his arrival at the hospital. Tragically, doctors stated that had a tourniquet been applied to Messenger's leg wounds, he would probably

Shutford, 1955, twenty years after the murders. (Author's collection)

Shutford as it looks today. (© N. Sly)

The barn from which the fatal shots were fired. (© N. Sly)

have survived. His brother was seriously injured and it looked likely that his leg would have to be amputated.

An inquest was opened into the deaths by the coroner for North Oxfordshire, Mr E.C. Fortescue. Although the three bus passengers, who had been taken to Horton Hospital at Banbury, had died outside his jurisdiction, he had arranged with the coroner for Banbury to conduct the inquest on all four of the deceased.

It emerged that Hilda Gibbs had been married to Wilfred for three years and they had one child, a little boy. The family had lived together in a cottage opposite the home of Wilfred's father, Sidney Gibbs, but ten days before the shooting, Wilfred had left his cottage with his baby son and moved back with his father. There had been problems in the couple's marriage and both Wilfred and Hilda had consulted solicitors, although their separation hadn't progressed any further than Wilfred moving out of the marital home and no legal proceedings had yet been initiated by either of the couple.

Although Hilda continued to live at the cottage directly opposite her husband's father's home, she had not seen her baby since Wilfred moved out. Wilfred, on the other hand, had kept a very close eye on Hilda, whom he was said to love dearly. He had spent time listening outside her windows and had also threatened her with a shotgun, at which she had told him not to be a fool. On the evening of her murder, he had borrowed his father's car and deliberately followed the bus on an earlier journey to ascertain whether or not his wife was a passenger. When he established that she wasn't, he returned to Shutford and went to the dance at the fête, where he was seen only ten minutes before the shootings occurred.

Hilda, who was distraught without her baby, had tried several times to recover the child from her husband, who believed that she was taking the baby with her to the pub and had therefore asked his mother to look after his son, saying, 'I do not want him to be where there is an influence of drink.'

Before too long, both Hilda and Wilfred's parents were dragged into the marital discord between their children. Hilda's father, Walter Goode, had gone with her to a property owned by Wilfred's grandfather to try and recover the baby, but the boy had not been there. Walter had also remonstrated with Wilfred after he had threatened Hilda with the shotgun but said that Wilfred, who stood over 6ft tall and was known as a 'gentle giant', was too much of a coward to face him. He had therefore made an official complaint to the police about Wilfred's conduct.

Walter also believed that Wilfred's mother had interfered in the marriage and that if she had '… kept out and allowed Hilda to have the baby as she was entitled to', then things could have been worked out. Mrs Gibbs senior denied having known anything about her son's marital discord until two weeks before the tragedy. In an interview with the *Oxford Mail*, she revealed that her son's neighbours had known of the young couple's troubles but had not spoken out. 'For this last year, his marriage has been a misery but my son never told me or his father anything about it,' she told reporters, adding that she wished her son's neighbours had said something so that she might have helped her son.

Wilfred's father, Sidney, admitted that his son had felt some jealousy over Hilda but insisted that Wilfred loved his child passionately and didn't want the boy to remain with her because he believed she was taking the child with her when she went drinking. This was immediately denied by Hilda's father, who described his daughter as 'too straight' to even contemplate taking the baby into a public house.

Sidney Gibbs then told the inquest that charges had been made against his son by a local girl but after Wilfred had consulted a solicitor, the charges were immediately dropped. Gibbs did not specify the exact nature of these charges and, as they had come to nothing, he was spared the embarrassment of having to elaborate further.

Denying that his son was of a cruel, murderous or violent nature, Sidney Gibbs stated that on more than one occasion, Hilda had come to his house after Wilfred had moved out, to try and get her baby. On one of these occasions, she had struck Wilfred in the face six times but he had not retaliated. On another, Hilda had used such insulting language that Sidney had warned her to leave his premises. When she had not done so, he had thrown two buckets of water over her.

Once, Gibbs had found his son sleeping in one of his stables and, when he asked him why he was there, Wilfred replied, 'There was going to be a row and I walked away.'

The inquest heard from the passengers on the bus as well as the driver, conductor and several passers-by. All told exactly the same story of two shots being fired from a cowshed, followed by a third shot, then silence. The gun used was an old service rifle that had belonged to Sidney Gibbs. He had bought it after the war, sixteen or seventeen years previously, and had since kept it at the back of an old cupboard in his kitchen, behind some rubbish. Gibbs told the inquest that he hadn't realised that anyone knew it was there, although he admitted that his son knew that there were cartridges stored in a bureau in the house. These were old French and German cartridges dating back to around 1903, which Sidney Gibbs had bought while he was serving in the Yeomanry and Artillery before the war. Two of the cartridges – one live and one blank – had been found in the bedroom that Wilfred Gibbs had been using at his father's house, along with the three found in the cowshed.

Dr Briggs testified that he had been Mrs Gibbs's regular doctor and that she had told him that she was unhappily married and that her husband had taken her child and she didn't know where her baby was. Questioned by the coroner, Dr Briggs agreed that the hot weather might have affected Wilfred Gibbs and that it was also a possibility that Gibbs might have been 'driven temporarily out of his wits' by jealousy.

The verdict of the coroner's jury was a foregone conclusion. They determined that Hilda Gibbs, Ivy Goode and Joseph Messenger had been murdered by Wilfred Gibbs who had then committed *felo de se* (self murder or suicide). However, if the verdict was easily decided, the one question that couldn't be answered so readily was Gibbs's motive for destroying a woman he was said to love deeply and then committing suicide, leaving his beloved child motherless and fatherless. Gibbs was a man who would always walk away from an argument and who was known in the village of Shutford as 'a quiet, reserved and sober man', from a respectable family.

MOTHER'S SUSPICION OF MARITAL UNHAPPINESS IN 1934

"Neighbours Knew, But They Never Spoke of the Trouble. I Wish They Had"

SECRET DIVULGED

"I am Sure it is the Scandal That Preyed on His Mind"

A special "Oxford Mail" photograph of Mrs. Hilda Gibbs.

NEW LIGHT ON THE TRAGEDY AT SHUTFORD, IN THE EXTREME NORTH OF OXFORDSHIRE, WHERE ON SATURDAY EVENING A 25-YEAR-OLD VILLAGE BLACKSMITH IS ALLEGED TO HAVE SHOT HIS WIFE AND TWO OTHER PEOPLE DEAD AND WOUNDED ANOTHER MAN, BEFORE SHOOTING HIMSELF DEAD, WAS THROWN BY THE STORY TOLD TO THE "OXFORD MAIL" TO-DAY BY MRS. GIBBS MOTHER OF THE MAN SAID TO HAVE FIRED THE SHOTS

A newspaper article reporting on the Shutford murders. (By kind permission of the Oxford Mail *and the* Oxford Times)

In the words of Dr John Alexander, who examined Gibbs's body after his death and could find no organic abnormalities, it was just possible that, under the circumstances, Gibbs might have had a sudden brainstorm. Ironically, just hours before gunning down his wife, his sister-in-law and two total strangers, Wilfred Gibbs had attended the village fête and won several prizes during the day for clay pigeon shooting.

Note: In various contemporary newspaper accounts of the shootings, there are conflicting reports on the reasons behind the Messenger brothers' presence on the bus. Some newspapers state that they had visited the fête and stayed too long, others report that the brothers had been to Banbury, shopping for a birthday present for their mother, who would have been seventy years old on the day after the tragedy.

25

'I HAD BETTER CONFESS. I AM GUILTY'

Oxford, 1938

If it were at all possible for a person to simply vanish into thin air then it seemed as though sixteen-year-old Harold Matthews had done just that. For two terms, Matthews, who was described by his mother as '...one of the nicest and best behaved boys any mother could wish to have', had been working as a pantry boy at Wycliffe Hall, the theological training college in Banbury Road, Oxford, where he was known as 'a bright, cheerful lad' and a good worker. Part of Harold's duties involved taking telephone calls and on Saturday, 5 February 1938, he was busy cleaning knives in the pantry when, at about 12.15 p.m., he was called upstairs to answer the telephone. He was expected to return to his work within minutes and, when he didn't come back to the pantry, an immediate search was made of the college premises. However, his worried colleagues could find no trace of him.

Harold's family and the police were notified that he was missing and, fearing that the boy may have suffered a sudden brainstorm or temporary loss of memory, a further search of the college premises was made. When there was still no sign of the young pantry boy, the search area was expanded to take in the college grounds and, later, the streets and parks in the immediate area. It wasn't until the following day that a student found Harold's naked and mutilated body lying on a level part of the roof of a building, used by the students as an open-air dormitory in the summer. The only access to the roof area was through a window in a small room, serviced by a

Wycliffe Hall, where Harold Matthews worked. (© N. Sly)

narrow stairway, and the police were of the opinion that the body had been pushed out of the window onto the roof.

Having recovered the boy's body, the police asked Home Office pathologist Dr James Matthewson Webster to perform a post-mortem examination. Webster found that Harold had died from asphyxiation, having been strangled with a ligature, and estimated the time of his death to have been at around 2.30 p.m. on 5 February. He noted the presence of additional ligature marks around Harold's wrists and ankles, which suggested that the boy had been tied up for some time before his death. There were several superficial bruises on both sides of Harold's head, along with a deeper bruise just above his left ear and whatever had caused that bruise could have rendered him unconscious. He had a black eye and abrasions on his chin, left cheek and at the base of his nose. There were six puncture wounds on his right breast and a further three on his left breast, with a 6in gash on his right flank. Webster concluded that, when the ligature had been applied to Harold's neck, the boy had either been unconscious or stunned and so unable to resist.

The police conducted a detailed search of the area around the access to the roof and found a nearby cupboard with a sizeable pool of blood on the floor. Alive or dead, Harold had obviously been placed in this cupboard, so the police began their enquiries by interviewing the three students who had rooms on the same landing. When the first student, John Stanley Phillips, was asked if he could throw any light on the death of the pantry boy, he immediately said, 'I had better confess. I am guilty.'

Phillips then asked to see the college principal, Mr J.R. Strickland Taylor, and, having consulted with him for a few minutes turned to Chief Constable Mr C.R. Fox and told him, 'I have nothing to say except that I am guilty. No one assisted me in it. It was not even premeditated. I did this about half past twelve yesterday, when I returned from the post office.'

Phillips was taken to the police station where he produced a quantity of trouser buttons and a pair of braces belonging to the victim, which he told the police that he had tried unsuccessfully to burn. His wallet contained a safety razor blade and when Phillips's rooms at the college were searched, the police found abundant evidence. The interior of his travelling trunk was heavily bloodstained, as was a sheet, which was recovered from an attaché case. In the grate in the bedroom was an 11in long piece of cord and there was ash in the grate in the living room, which appeared to consist of the remains of burned cord and clothing. A walking stick in Phillips's bedroom was stained with blood on one end and there were also spots of blood on a pair of his grey flannel trousers and on his pyjamas, as well as on several of his handkerchiefs.

An inquest was opened into the death of Harold Matthews and lasted only for a couple of minutes before being adjourned. Harold's identity was formally confirmed by his father, Ernest Matthews, who had already undergone the unenviable task of viewing his son's body at the city mortuary. The man charged with his murder, John Phillips, was the son of a clergyman from Woking. He was twenty-one years old and had already gained a BA degree at Selwyn College, Cambridge, before coming to Wycliffe Hall to study for holy orders. A slightly built, fair-haired man with gold-rimmed glasses, Phillips sat through the short inquest with his head bowed, listening as Chief Constable Fox stated that he would be passing the case to the Director of Public Prosecutions.

Harold Matthews. (By kind permission of the Oxford Mail *and the* Oxford Times*)*

Phillips was later to appear before magistrates H.S. Rogers, A.M. Eagleston and J.S. Chaundler at Oxford, charged with the wilful murder of Harold Matthews. At the commencement of the proceedings, Mr Rogers, the Mayor of Oxford and chairman of the magistrates, 'noted with regret' the presence of a large number of ladies in court. While acknowledging that they had a perfect right to be there, he suggested that some of the details they might hear would not be suitable for their ears and appealed to their good sense to leave the court. Most of the women present obediently left before the business of the hearing began.

Committed for trial by the magistrates for the charge of murder against him, Phillips appeared at the Central Criminal Court, or Old Bailey, on 6 April 1938 before Mr Justice Asquith. The case was prosecuted by Mr G.B. McClure, while Norman Birkett KC appeared in defence of Phillips, who pleaded 'Not Guilty'.

Once the prosecution had outlined the case and introduced their witnesses, Birkett informed the court that the defence was not disputing the fact that Phillips had committed the murder with which he was charged. However, Birkett told the jury that he would be asking them to return a verdict of 'Guilty but insane' against his client.

One of the first witnesses called by the defence was the Reverend Stanley Phillips, the vicar of St Mary's Church in Woking, Surrey. Mr Phillips assured the court that, as a child, his son had never given him a moment's anxiety and stated that no father could ever speak more highly of his son, whose ambition in life was to become a foreign missionary. However, Mr Phillips senior had noticed lately that his son's religious beliefs seemed very intense and, although John was very keen, his outlook was somewhat narrow. John's father related that his son had believed it wrong to take a bath on a Sunday and that he had abhorred entertainments such as cinemas as being inexpedient and unwholesome. Recently, he had become reserved and secretive and had completely withdrawn from all social activities.

Birkett then called Dr H. Yellowlees, a Harley Street psychiatrist who had visited Phillips while he was remanded in Brixton Prison and formed the opinion that the defendant was suffering from schizophrenia. He described the disease as a 'splitting of the mind', in which the concepts of right and wrong simply did not exist. Yellowlees had found Phillips to be bored and disinterested, even slightly peevish, at their meeting, likening him to a child whose play had been interrupted to be brought into the drawing room to listen to the polite conversation of grown-ups.

Nevertheless, Phillips was willing to answer questions about the murder and, when Yellowlees asked him how he had been spending his time in custody Phillips told him that he had been reliving the murder, trying to think out how he might have carried it out more successfully. Phillips related what Yellowlees called 'a dream story', in which he confessed to having fantasised about finding a person whose identity was of no importance and cutting off that person's arms and legs. Phillips was under the impression that this could be done without killing his selected victim, after which he intended to keep the dismembered trunk and play with it. If he left college, he would simply take the body with him.

Birkett questioned Yellowlees about the disease of schizophrenia, which the doctor informed him was an illness of slow origin and development.

Birkett then called Dr Grierson, the medical officer at Brixton Prison, who had observed Phillips in custody from 9 March onwards. Grierson did not consider Phillips to be insane, although he conceded that he was certainly not a person of 'normal mind', saying that he had shown no remorse whatsoever for what he had done. Yet Grierson could not agree that Phillips had not known what he was doing at the time of the murder.

It was then left to Mr Justice Asquith to sum up the evidence for the jury. There were three possible verdicts, said Asquith – 'Not Guilty', 'Guilty' and 'Guilty but insane' – and the prosecution had established beyond any reasonable doubt that the first of these did not apply. Therefore the verdict was a simple choice between the latter two options.

The judge reminded the jury that the defendant had been described as intensely and narrowly religious and also as unsociable and reserved by nature. He had shown no remorse, fear or any other trace of emotion after the murder and had continued to behave in what was, for him, a perfectly normal manner. On the day after the murder, he went to Holy Communion and on the morning of the murder itself he had attended church in Oxford, appearing quite normal to all those who had observed him. The defence had not disputed Phillips's guilt but had instead pushed for a verdict of 'Guilty but insane'.

'What insanity would justify that verdict?' asked Asquith, going on to explain that abnormality was not enough and neither was certifiable insanity. What the defence sought to establish was that, by reason of a disease of the mind, at the time of the offence Phillips did not know that what he was doing was wrong.

Dr Yellowlees was a highly qualified expert in such diseases and it was his professional opinion that the defendant was suffering from schizophrenia or a forerunner of the disease, *dementia praecox*. He defined the symptoms of the illness as an unnatural emotional indifference – as living in two worlds, one of fantasy and the other of dissociation. Either Phillips's behaviour was the very clever play-acting of someone who was pretending to be mad or it was a genuine abnormality of the mind and Yellowlees believed that it was the latter.

The jury deliberated for only a few minutes before returning a verdict of 'Guilty but insane', at which the judge directed that Phillips should be detained until his Majesty's pleasure should be known.

No evidence of any prior relationship between Phillips and his victim was ever found. Tragically it appeared that the young pantry boy had just been unfortunate enough to encounter someone whose hitherto undiagnosed mental illness had turned him from a quiet, reserved and studious man to an emotionless killer, who was completely incapable of following the doctrine of his own strictly-held religious beliefs.

26

'SHE DARED ME TO DO IT'

Horley, 1952

At 3.30 p.m. on 19 May 1952, a distressed young man approached a railway signal box at Moor Hill near Horley and asked the signal man, Arthur Phipps, to telephone for the police as he had just murdered a girl. By the time PC Robinson arrived in response to the call, the man was sobbing bitterly.

'She dared me to do it,' he told the police tearfully, pointing to where the body of twenty-one-year-old Rose Margaret Meadows lay beneath a hawthorn hedge in a field of buttercups, about 250 yards from the Horley to Hanwell road and less than half a mile from the safety of her home in Horley. A later post-mortem examination, conducted by Home Office pathologist Professor Webster, indicated that Miss Meadows had been manually strangled.

Detective Sergeant Robert Morgan immediately cautioned the man – Oliver George Butler – and arrested him on suspicion of the girl's murder. 'Nothing to say now,' said twenty-four-year-old Butler, yet by the time he reached Banbury police station, he had undergone an apparent change of heart and willingly made a detailed statement.

He and Miss Meadows were both employed at 'the Ally' – the Northern Aluminium Co. Ltd works in Southam Road, Banbury. They had been sweethearts and were very much in love, in spite of the fact that Butler already had a wife. He had somehow managed to convince both Rose and her mother, Ethel, that he would soon be getting a divorce and would then be free to marry Rose. He had seemed so sincere that Ethel had willingly allowed him to move into her house. (She was later to describe her daughter and Butler as being 'desperately in love'.)

Horley, home of Rose Margaret Meadows. (© N. Sly)

According to Butler, Rose had been obsessed by death and had frequently talked of murder and suicide. Whenever Rose turned the conversation towards such a morbid subject, Butler said he always told her to stop it and not be silly but Rose had been sure that it was her destiny to be murdered – she had been told of her ultimate fate by a fortune teller and had always insisted that, if she was going to be murdered, she would rather be murdered by Butler than by anybody else.

On 19 May, the couple set out for an afternoon walk and stopped to make love in the woods. In the aftermath of their lovemaking, Rose remarked that this would be a good place for a murder. She then went on to talk about their relationship, telling Butler that she was convinced that he would go back to his wife one day and, when that happened, she would have to find another boyfriend.

Butler told her that, if she left him for another man, it would make him feel like murdering her. He told the police that he believed Rose was trying to 'work him up' and that he had placed his hands around her throat with the intention of frightening her. 'I was not being serious,' he insisted, but Rose had sneered and laughed at him and goaded him to get on with it, saying that she had heard Butler's wife say that she would never give him a divorce.

'I got mad,' Butler's statement continued. 'I did not intend anything should part us.' He then claimed that he must have accidentally squeezed her throat too hard, as she collapsed and died almost instantly.

Brought before magistrates at Banbury, charged with the wilful murder of Rose Meadows, Butler was committed for trial at the next assizes. He appeared at Stafford Assizes on 4 July 1952, before Mr Justice Hallett. Mr E. Ryder Richardson prosecuted, while Butler, who pleaded 'Not Guilty', was defended by Mr G.G. Baker.

Butler was sticking very firmly to his original statement, that Miss Meadows had frequently talked of murder and believed that it was her destiny to die in that fashion. Her death, insisted Butler, had been a terrible accident – one that had only occurred because she had egged him on and dared him to do it.

However, by the time the case came to trial, Butler had added a new twist to his defence and now tried to convince the court that Rose Meadows had a weak heart. The prosecution called Mrs Ethel Eliza Meadows and Miss Iris Lucy Meadows – Rose's mother and sister – to ask them about Rose's health.

Both strenuously denied that Rose had ever complained of any heart trouble. Mr Baker cross-examined both, asking Iris Meadows directly if Rose had ever mentioned having a weak heart to her.

'No,' Iris said firmly.

Baker asked her if she recalled going on a roundabout with her sister at Banbury Fair and Rose being ill when she got off the ride.

'No. I cannot remember,' insisted Iris.

Baker tried to hammer the point home, asking Iris if she had told Rose that she was silly to go on the roundabout with her heart 'like that'.

'I never said it,' Iris replied.

It was then left to Butler to argue some of the finer points of his initial statement to the police. He told the court that when he had said 'I got mad', what he actually meant was that he was 'frustrated'. If he was mad with anybody it was with his wife rather than Rose, whom he professed to have loved very much indeed.

When he asked for the police to be summoned because he had 'murdered' his girlfriend, he had been too upset to think properly and had not thought to say that there had been a terrible accident. He told the court that he couldn't remember using the phrase 'I did not intend anything should part us' in his statement, saying that what he meant to say was, 'I do not intend anything should part us' – words that were supposed to express his intention to commit suicide now that his beloved Rose was dead.

In his summary of the evidence for the jury, Mr Justice Hallett told them:

It may well be you will think that this is as plain a case as you are ever likely to find of intentional murder and intentional confession. You may think this is one of those cases of plain, obvious murder, a plain, unambiguous confession and later, when the man's courage fails, he takes back that confession in a desperate, futile attempt to explain away the murder.

The jury was unconvinced by Butler's arguments, particularly the more recent embellishment to his statement that the dead woman's alleged heart condition was a contributory factor to her death. Neither Rose's mother nor her sister had been aware

Oxford Prison, now a hotel. (© N. Sly)

that she had suffered from any such physical defect and nor had the post-mortem examination revealed any inherent weakness. The jury found Butler guilty as charged and Mr Justice Hallett pronounced the mandatory death sentence. However, some small part of Butler's evidence must have rung true with the jury, since their verdict was surprisingly accompanied by a strong recommendation for mercy.

Butler's defence counsel went on to appeal the verdict on the grounds that Mr Justice Hallett had misdirected the jury by telling them that it was a case of murder, whereas it was the contention of the defence that, since Butler had not meant to kill her but only to frighten her, Miss Meadows's death occurred as the result of an accident. The appeal was heard on 28 July at the Court of Criminal Appeal before the Lord Chief Justice, Mr Justice Hilbery and Mr Justice Slade.

After consideration of the evidence, the Lord Chief Justice delivered the court's judgement. In trying to frighten Miss Meadows by placing his hands around her throat, the appeal judges believed that Butler was 'pursuing an unlawful object', in a way that he knew would be likely to result in her death. In the opinion of the appeal court, Butler's own evidence had shown that Miss Meadows' death was murder and they were confident that the trial judge had directed the jury properly. Thus Butler's appeal was dismissed and, with it, any hope of a reprieve. Oliver George Butler was hanged on 12 August 1952, becoming the last person ever to be executed at Oxford Prison.

27

'I WAS THERE AND YET
I WASN'T'

Oxford, 1963

On 18 October 1963, fifteen-year-old Glenys Mary Jewell left her home in Albert Street, Jericho, at about five o'clock in the afternoon, telling her parents that she had a date.

Dressed in black ski pants and a brown suedette jacket, Glenys first went to the local recreation ground, where she was seen by her brothers, Melvyn and John, talking to three other girls. Then, as far as Mr and Mrs Jewell were aware, their daughter was intending to go to the Scala Cinema in Oxford, where the Indian film *Two Daughters* was being screened and indeed, she was seen leaving the cinema later that evening by her eighteen-year-old brother, Michael. At that time, she was accompanied by a man, who Michael didn't recognise.

When Glenys didn't return home that night, her parents reported her missing and the police began an extensive search for the teenager. By 3 November, when she still hadn't been found, they called for volunteers to mount a methodological search, intending to cover a 1 mile radius from the Carfax area of Oxford.

The police were overwhelmed with the response to their appeal as more than 1,500 people turned out to scour the area. They included Gurkhas who were training at Abingdon, the fire brigade, members of the RAF and the Territorial Army, senior scouts, schoolboys from St Edward's School and hundreds of civilians, including friends and neighbours of the missing girl. Glenys's father and two older brothers, John and Michael, also joined in the search, although her father later commented to reporters, 'I was hoping and praying that I wouldn't find her.' Thirteen-year-old Melvyn also tried to join the search party but was intercepted by a policeman and told that he was too young. 'But it's my sister they are looking for,' he protested, but

Carfax and High Street, Oxford. (Author's collection)

to no avail. He was placed in the charge of a policewoman, who gave him tea and sandwiches while the search continued without him.

The police divided the searchers into twelve parties, each one led by a senior police officer equipped with a walkie-talkie radio, with a direct link to a control room that had been set up at police headquarters. The local Round Table arranged transport for the searchers, while the WRVS manned a series of tea vans, keeping the volunteers supplied with hot drinks. The searchers diligently combed every part of their designated areas, walking through open ground, churchyards and cemeteries, peering into sheds and outbuildings and logging every unoccupied house or building they came across on their routes.

The search began at 9.30 a.m. and, within a short time, a message crackled over the walkie-talkie system to say that one of the parties had found discarded woman's clothing.

Police rushed to investigate but soon established that the clothing was not connected to the missing girl. Soon afterwards, a woman's handbag was found in a semi-derelict house in Cranham Street but the police were quickly able to eliminate it from the investigation.

Just before noon, two parties who had been searching the university area of the city met up and joined forces. A few of them headed down a private road in Holywell Ford to investigate the allotments there and one just happened to glance over a wall, spotting a shoe and a pair of slacks.

Clerk Adrian Pattison called over one of the policemen supervising his party and pointed out the clothes to him, before continuing his search of the allotments. Under a heap of vegetation, he found the partly clothed body of a young woman, later identified by the suedette jacket and a gilt bangle she was wearing as being that of Glenys Jewell.

The police immediately cleared the area and erected a tarpaulin over the body. The Chief Constable of Oxford, Mr C.G. Burrows and his deputy, Superintendent Leonard

North, were both part of the search for the missing girl and were quickly summoned to the scene of the grim discovery, along with police surgeon Dr Graeme McFarlane. Later, City Coroner Mr T.E. Gardiner and Home Office pathologist Dr D.F. Barrowcliffe arrived and supervised the removal of Glenys's body to the mortuary in Floyd's Row. A post-mortem examination was carried out by Barrowcliffe and McFarlane, with Dr W.E. Montgomery, the director of the West Midland Forensic Science Laboratory in attendance. It was determined that Glenys had been strangled by ligature.

At first light the next morning, the police began a fingertip search of the allotments as well as interviewing the holders of each individual plot. One man, Mr Daniel Dunn, told police that he had been working on his allotment only days earlier and had passed within 2ft of the pile of runner beans, Michaelmas daisies and leaves, beneath which Glenys had been discovered. At the time, he had seen nothing unusual and told police that the compost did not appear to have been disturbed in any way. Meanwhile police issued an appeal to the public through the local press, asking for anyone who had seen Glenys with a man in the Holywell area to come forward. They also appealed to taxi drivers who might have either picked up Glenys and her male companion, or carried a lone male fare from Holywell.

Within days, the local newspaper carried a small, seemingly insignificant report of a man who had been arrested in the city for theft. Twenty-six-year-old Patrick Michael Breen, a married man from Old Marston, appeared before magistrates charged with breaking and entering a house and stealing traveller's cheques, Post Office Savings Bank books and other papers. There was a further charge of receiving papers and envelopes between 7 and 29 October, knowing them to have been stolen, and finally a charge of stealing by finding the sum of £42, belonging to some person or persons unknown, on a date unknown.

At his appearance before magistrates, Breen was remanded in custody until 12 November, despite the fact that his father-in-law was prepared to stand bail for him. Unusually for such relatively minor offences, the police strongly opposed bail. 'At this stage, I will say no more,' commented Deputy Chief Constable Leonard North when questioned about this decision. The reason for his reticence was soon to become obvious when Breen was later charged with the wilful murder of Glenys Mary Jewell.

Having been arrested on 29 October, Breen was routinely questioned about Glenys Jewell and readily told the police that he had seen her on the night of her disappearance. According to Breen, he had briefly met Glenys in Friar's Entry at 7.15 p.m. She had said 'Hello' and walked with him to the Gloucester Arms public house, which he entered alone. When he came out again half an hour later, Glenys was still outside. Breen told the police that they had gone to a milk bar in Gloucester Street, where he had left Glenys alone and gone to the Nag's Head public house, arriving there at 8 p.m.

As police made further enquiries into the chance meetings between Breen and the murdered girl, they received several interesting pieces of information that eventually led to Breen being charged with the murder. A taxi driver came forward to say that she had taken Glenys and a man to the Scala cinema on the night of her disappearance.

The taxi driver later identified Glenys's male companion as Patrick Breen, as did a teenage friend of Glenys, who had seen her with a man in the city centre of Oxford.

A Mrs Brogan came forward to tell the police that Breen had spoken to her in the Duke of Edinburgh public house on 27 October and told her that he had met the missing girl on 18 October.

Breen's wife was interviewed and told the police that her husband had woken up in a cold sweat on the morning of Saturday 19 October. When she asked him what was wrong, he told her that he had dreamed he took Glenys along a towpath and then strangled her. While in custody, Breen had mentioned this dream to the police constable guarding his cell:

> I had a terrible dream that night, more of a nightmare. All I could see was her face. I was there and yet I wasn't. It was as though I was looking at myself doing something. I can't tell you what it was.

After several appearances before magistrates, Breen was committed for trial at the Berkshire Assizes, charged with Glenys's murder. His trial opened at Reading in January 1964 before Mr Justice Lawton.

The case for the prosecution was simple. Breen had been the last person to see Glenys Jewell alive therefore he must have strangled her. However, the defence, led by Mr R.V. Cusack QC maintained that the girl's death had been due to asphyxia resulting from a spasm of the glottis, caused by shock during sexual intercourse and that it had not been Breen who was with her at the time of her death. The jury chose to believe the prosecution's version of events and Breen was found 'Guilty', leading to a sentence of life imprisonment being passed by Mr Justice Lawton.

Soon after the end of the trial, Breen's solicitors were approached by a controversial new witness. Patrick Brian Flanagan had been in prison in Oxford during the magistrates' court appearances and the trial and had thus not been able to testify. Now he stated that he had seen Glenys in the ABC cinema on the night of her disappearance in the company of a man who was definitely not Patrick Breen. Moreover, having left the cinema, he had also seen Breen alone in the Nag's Head public house.

Flanagan stated that he had known Glenys Jewell since she was a child and that on 18 October he had been to see a film at the ABC

The Gloucester Arms. (© N. Sly)

cinema. Glenys and her male companion had taken a seat three rows in front of him. Flanagan insisted that he had a clear view of Glenys when the cinema lights went up and Glenys briefly left the auditorium and walked to the ladies' room. Flanagan described the man with Glenys as having crew-cut hair and wearing a bomber jacket, likening him to an American serviceman. As the man was sitting in front of him, he had not seen his face but only the back of his head.

Flanagan and Breen had both been imprisoned at Oxford, although during their incarceration they had met only momentarily while both were queuing to see the governor. There had been no opportunity for any communication between the two men. Now Flanagan claimed to recognise Breen as a man he had seen drinking alone in the Nag's Head public house on the night of Glenys Jewell's disappearance, at a time when Flanagan had just left Glenys in the ABC cinema in the company of another man.

With potential new evidence in the case, Breen's defence team was granted leave to appeal his conviction. At the same time, Mr Cusack also complained about the judge's summing up in the original trial, claiming that it contained several inaccuracies that had ultimately proved prejudicial to his client.

The Court of Criminal Appeal led by the Lord Chief Justice, Lord Parker, with Mr Justice Stephenson and Mr Justice Widgery, granted Cusack's appeal to have the fresh evidence heard and, on 27 April 1964, the Appeal Court sat again under Lord Parker, Mr Justice Phillimore and Mr Justice Winn.

Counsel for the prosecution was given the opportunity to cross-examine the new defence witness, who repeated what he had told Breen's solicitors.

'You are not telling the truth, are you?' Flanagan was asked, at which he indignantly insisted that he was.

In the event, Flanagan's evidence was far from convincing, particularly in the light of sightings of the victim at or near the Scala cinema and the three appeal judges unanimously deemed it 'not capable of belief'. As a consequence, they saw no reason to interfere with the original sentence of life imprisonment passed upon Patrick Michael Breen after he had been found guilty of the murder of Glenys Mary Jewell.

Meanwhile, Glenys's grieving family applied to the local council to see if they could be moved from their home in Albert Street. 'We cannot face seeing Glenys's bedroom with all her records and pin-ups,' her devastated father told reporters.

Albert Street, where Glenys Jewell lived. (© N. Sly)

BIBLIOGRAPHY & REFERENCES

BOOKS

Brindley, Giles. *Oxford: Crime, Death and Debauchery*, Sutton Publishing, Stroud, 2006

Browne, Douglas G. and Tullett, E.V. *Bernard Spilsbury: His Life and Cases*, George G. Harrap and Co. Ltd, 1951

Eddleston, John J. *The Encyclopaedia of Executions*, John Blake, London, 2004

Fielding, Steve. *The Hangman's Record Volume One 1868-1899*, Chancery House Press, Beckenham, Kent, 1994

Woodley, Len. *Oxfordshire Murders*, Wychwood Press, Charlbury, 2005

NEWSPAPERS

Banbury Guardian
Jackson's Oxford Journal
London Evening Post
Manchester Guardian
News of the World
Oxford Chronicle
Oxford Mail
Oxford Times
Reading Evening Post
Reading Mercury
The Times

Various websites have also been consulted during the compilation of this book. However, since they have a tendency to disappear without notice, to avoid disappointment, they have not been individually listed.

INDEX